Art BC's

by

Dr. Marina Bichinsky &
Dr. Jane Goretskaya

ILLUSTRATED BY
STUDENTS OF
LivingArtStudio.ORG

Lifelong Approaches

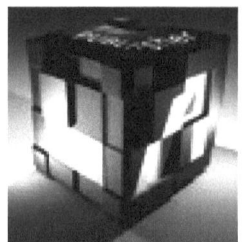

Publishing Group

With Living Art Studio

46923 Warm Springs Blvd., #104
Fremont, CA
Phone: 408.661.3634
www.LivingArtStudio.ORG

Email: marinabichinsky@yahoo.com

ISBN-13: 978-1482758443

ISBN-10: 148275844X

Welcome to the **ArtBC's** Learning Adventure!

Dear Parents!

Please do not miss a unique chance to participate in learning art activities that would help your children from the age of two to the middle school age learn Fine Art Basic while playing, seeing, and testing own skills.

Dr. Marina Bichinsky and Dr. Jane Goretskaya prepared this book to help your children cognitive and logical grow through play. The book includes drawings and paintings, created by your child's aged students in Living Art Studio in Fremont, California under their instructional leadership. Both authors are artists with the Master of Arts and Doctoral degrees with summative teaching experience of 50 years in European and American Art schools and Universities.

Enjoy, Share, Play, Act, Learn!

Welcome!
Dr. Marina Bichinsky
Dr. Jane Goretskaya

Dear Parents,

Welcome to the Art Learning Adventure!

What can you find in the learning environment of this book?

You may use this activity book to link art vocabulary with art images, designed by students of the Living Art Studio in Fremont, California. The authors of this book hope and believe that learning both the alphabet and vocabulary can introduce the child to the appreciation of art and perhaps willingness to start draw and paint something similar. Turning page by page along with a child, you, as a parent, would bring a child's attention to the shape and color of images, ask to repeat after you say the vocabulary on a page and attempt to make a little story of what is described by images, related by the first letter of the name or term. For instance, on the first page, you will meet the letter "A" that associates with such worlds as Artist and Apple. You will see pictures of two young artists, who have depicted flowers by using different techniques. Depending from the child experience or preferences, you may propose him or her to make piece similar to what Yannis did at age of 6, or like the complicated oil painting by Sabury, when she was just 12-years-old. The painting may be replaced by collage. Ask a child to use geometrical shapes to make flowers. The story should awake your child's imagination and be fun at the same time. Scenario may include the following:

Yan (you may use your child name) woke up at the morning and first what he saw was the blossoming Magnolia tree. Pedals of the flowers with red hearts on the tree were colored in light pink and looked like beautiful cups with some honey. You may ask a child: Do you know who likes the honey? Perhaps we can find this character on the next page. Ask a child: Do you want to meet him now or do you want to make a flower first?

Are you ready to go to other pages? Let's Go. Bon Voyage!

Dr Jane and Dr Marina here to help you discover the wonderland of painting.

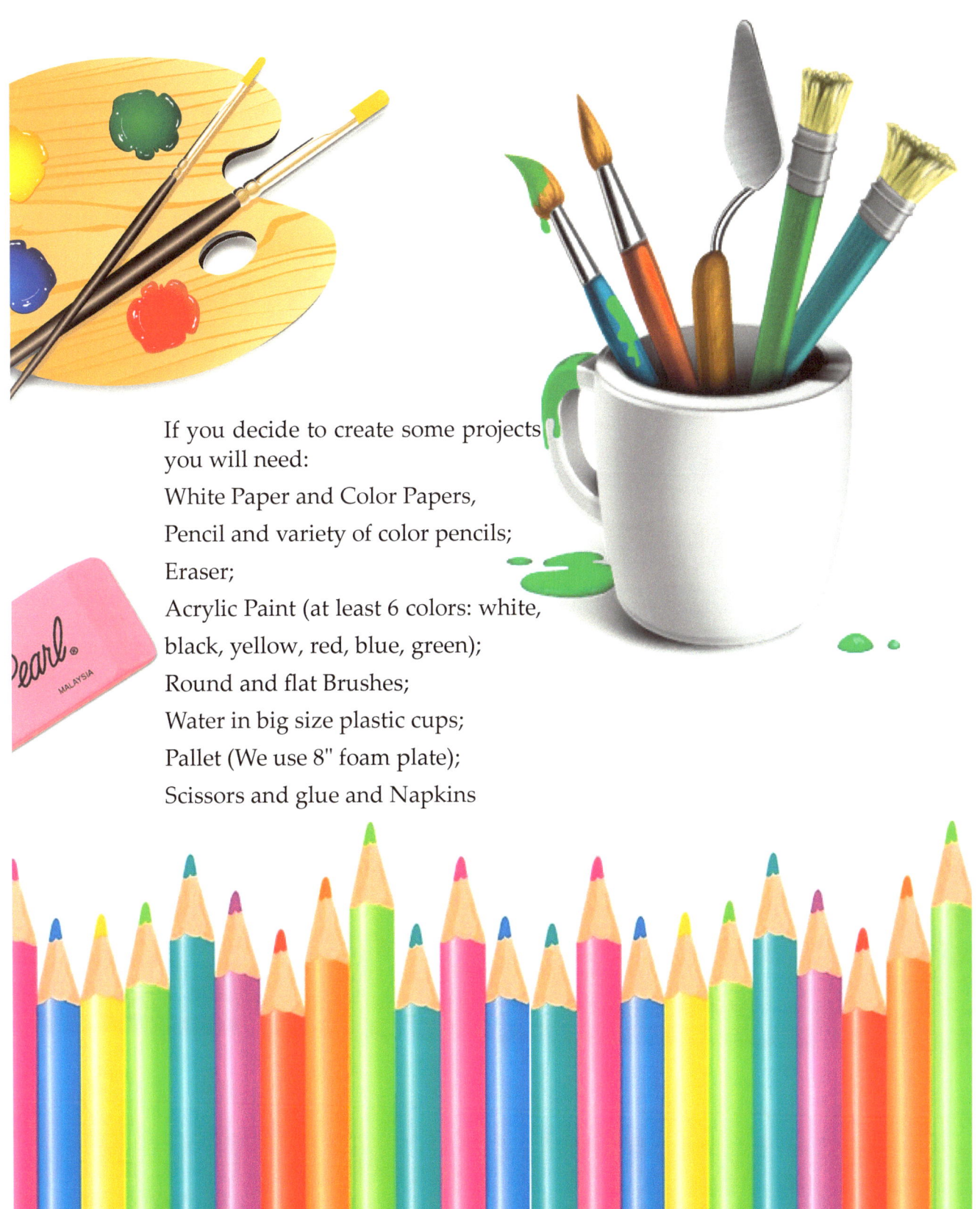

If you decide to create some projects you will need:

White Paper and Color Papers,

Pencil and variety of color pencils;

Eraser;

Acrylic Paint (at least 6 colors: white, black, yellow, red, blue, green);

Round and flat Brushes;

Water in big size plastic cups;

Pallet (We use 8" foam plate);

Scissors and glue and Napkins

Art
Artist
Apple

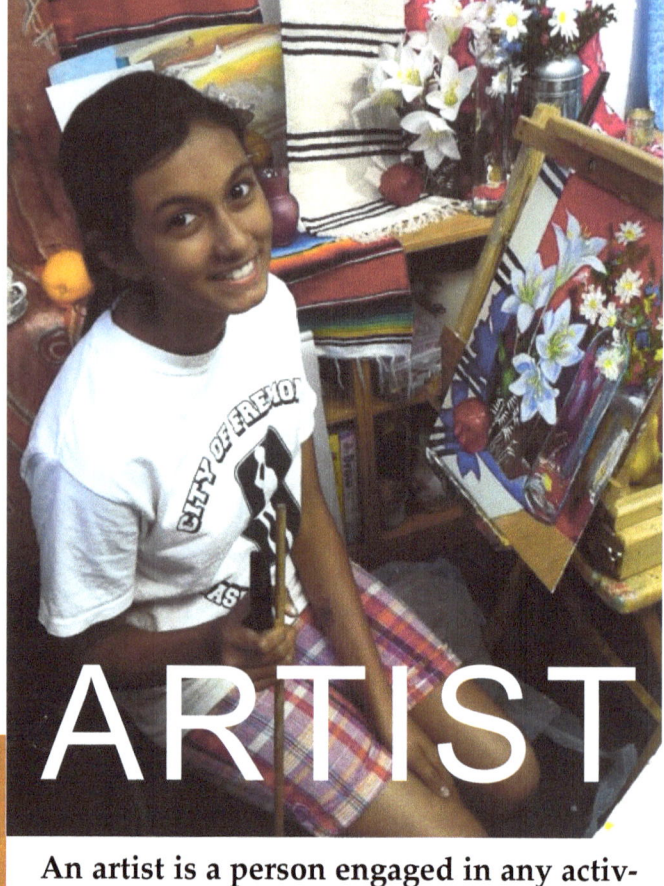

ARTIST

An artist is a person engaged in any activities related to creating art, practicing the arts, or demonstrating art.

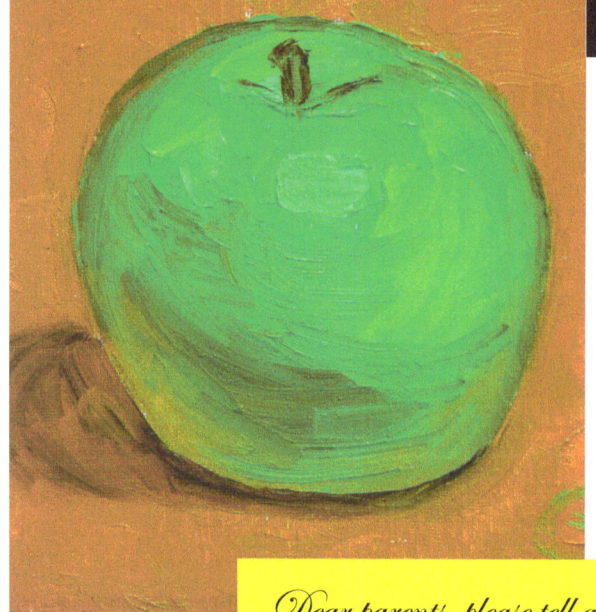

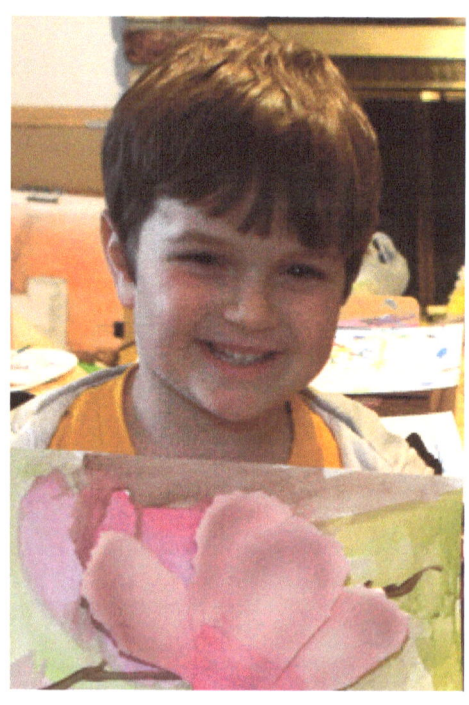

Dear parents, please tell a little story from your childhood's memory. Did you remember about your first trip to the art exhibition? Did you meet an artist there? Was this cool or boring?

Ann came in the Art class to learn how to draw flowers. What made Ann happy? She became an Artist. Let's discover what she depicted on her beautiful colorful painting. She learned how to do the background and flowers itself. What types of flowers Ann painted? A lily, daisies, corn-flowers, and even a rose. Could a child find on the background of her painting a color similar to color of the flowers? If so, please ask a child "How many red flowers and white flowers you can find in the painting. Could you find the same colors on the skirt and t-shirt that the young artist wore? What about the blue ones?" Please ask a child to draw his or her picture below.

BEAR

Blue

Bird

Brush

Avantika Vandanapu - age 6

Mihika - age 13

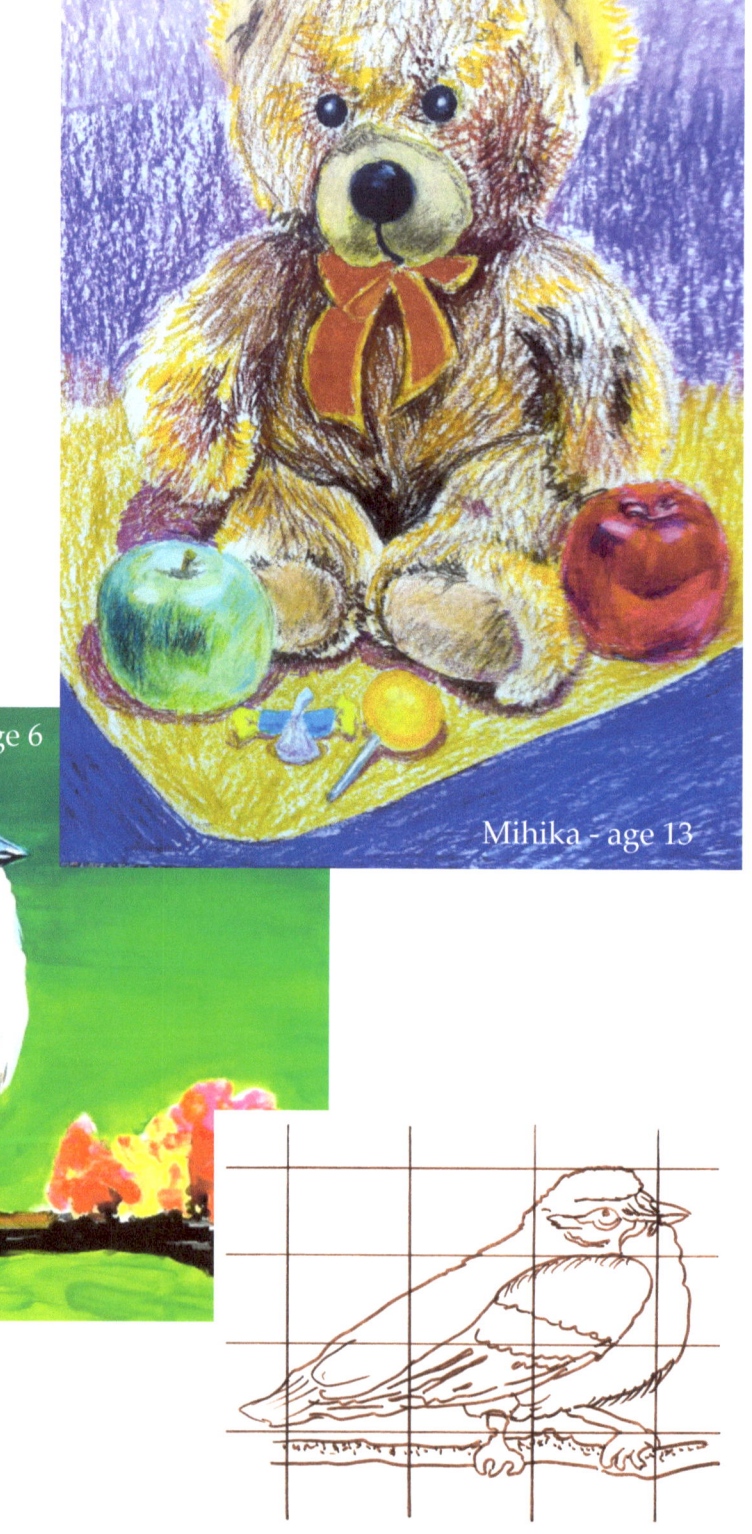

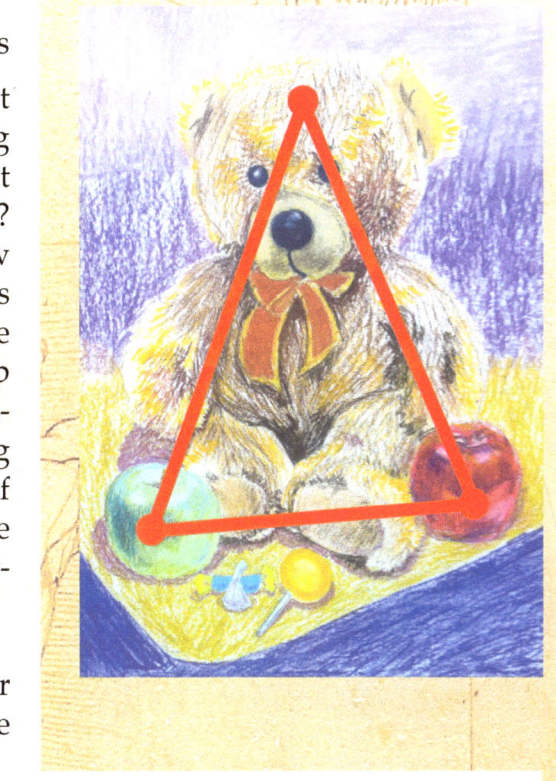

Could your child find a personage who likes honey? Indeed, it is a Bear. The young artist drew and painted this lovely Teddy Bear along with the fruits and candy. It looks like that it is a holiday or the Bear's birthday. Does it not? The artist used a triangle composition to show who is the major character on this painting. As you may see, the green and red apples create balance to show polar (contrast) relationship between the green and red colors and demonstrate friendly relationship without making them gray. A child may try to mix both of these colors on a separate white paper and see what will happen. Mixed color in 1:1 proportion would become gray.

The bird depicted on other picture and her song lets us know that spring is in the air. See how the artist has used brush strokes to show variety of the bird's feathers and fluffs on the winds, tail, head, and stomach. Ask a child to compare the size of the bird with her body. How many heads of the bird may be placed into her body? Despite that this question may sound slightly weird, in art, size of the body of any personage, including human, is always compared with the height of the head. Let's try to draw this bird with an open beak or with open wings on separate paper.

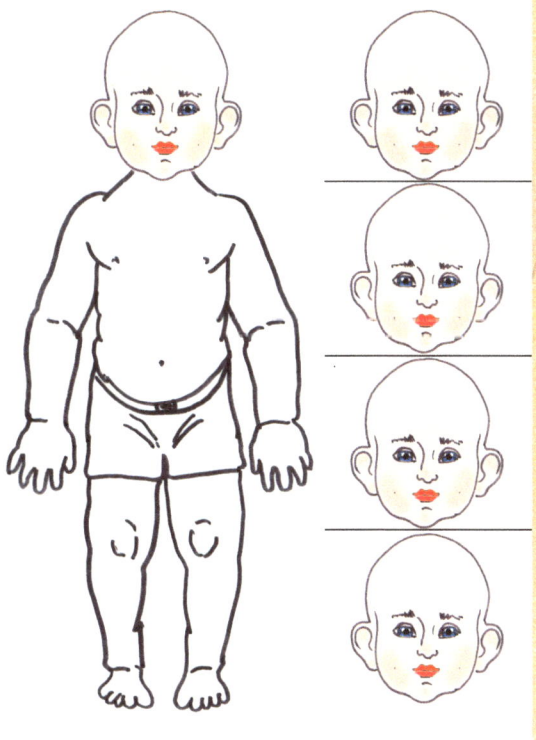

Cat

Dog and

Dalli

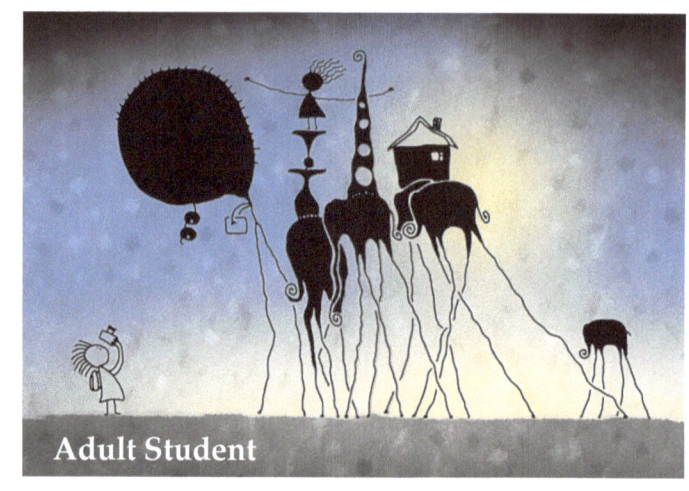

Adult Student

Susan Ron - age 8

The paintings on these pages represent relationships between small and big subjects. Despite the compositions are different, both artists use negative space to make connections between subjects. For instance, in the painting, depicting friendship between the cat and dog, the artist colored triangle between the two animals in dark brown. This negative space demonstrates their close friendly relationships.

Cup and Dasies

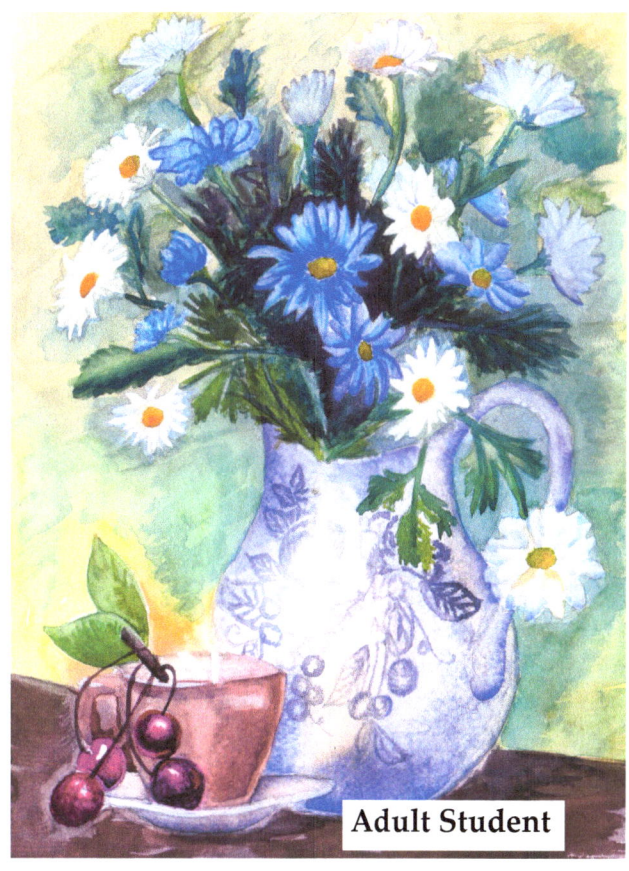

Adult Student

On the other painting, relationship between the beautiful cup and plate with lemon, made by two curved lines, has shown by negative space. Please bring a child's attention to the variety of colors on the cup's decor. The artist used these colors to keep entire composition in balance. Could you imagine what may happen if yellow sunny background would be replaced by a blue or a red one?

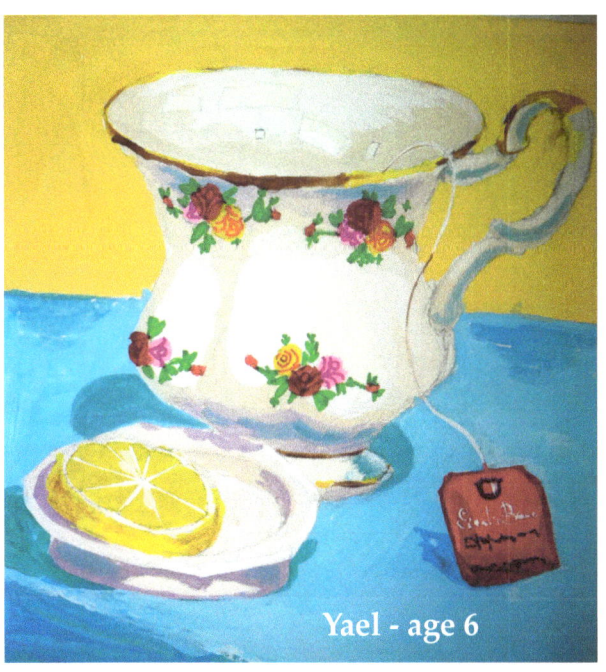

Yael - age 6

With the red background, the painting would describe the hours of the morning tea in the summer and will be immediately transformed to reflect dramatic view associated with the warning that tea is very hot and you need to wait for a while before starting sipping. You may ask a child to change background color on a separate paper to check what he or she think has happened in the room. The purpose of another exercise is to find negative spaces in the painting between flowers and cherries. This exercise would bring good experience and clear understanding of what the negative space is about.

Eagle, **E**asel, & a copy of **E**sher's

drawing are united by the letter "**E**". Similar to the eagle wings, which help him fly by moving wings up and down, Esher's drawing reflects metaphor that the hands may be seen also as up and down wings that help people create.

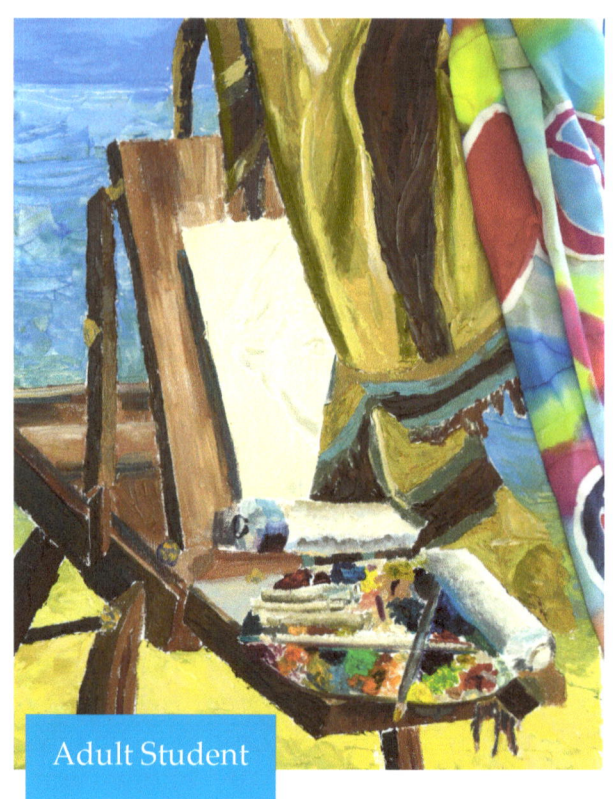

Adult Student

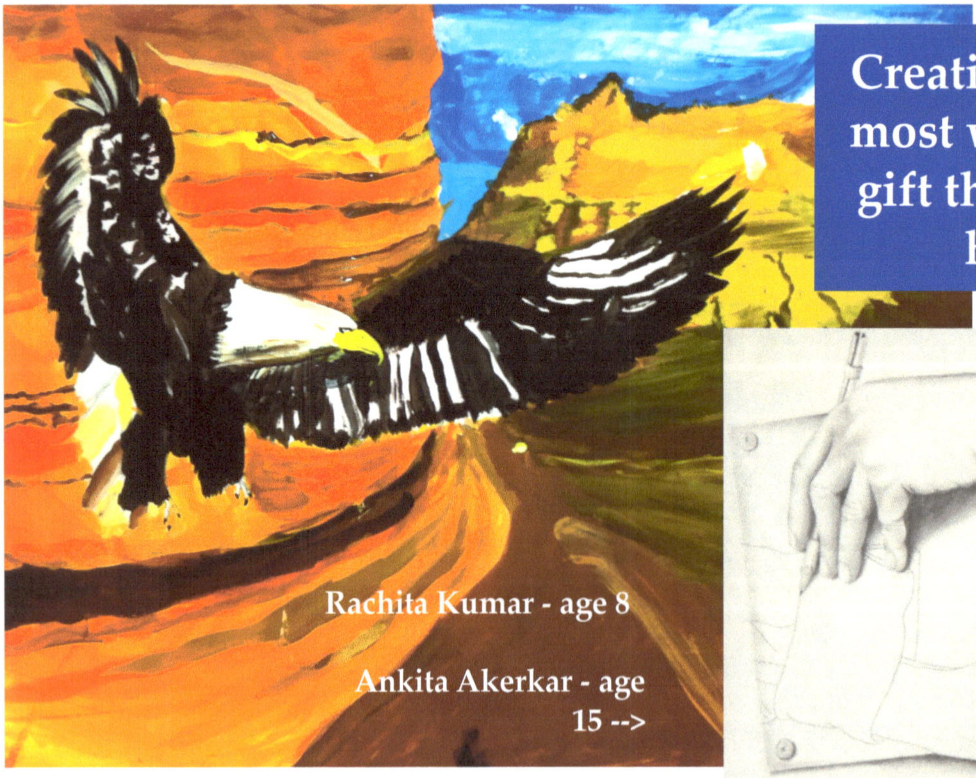

Creativity is the most wonderful gift that people have.

Rachita Kumar - age 8

Ankita Akerkar - age 15 -->

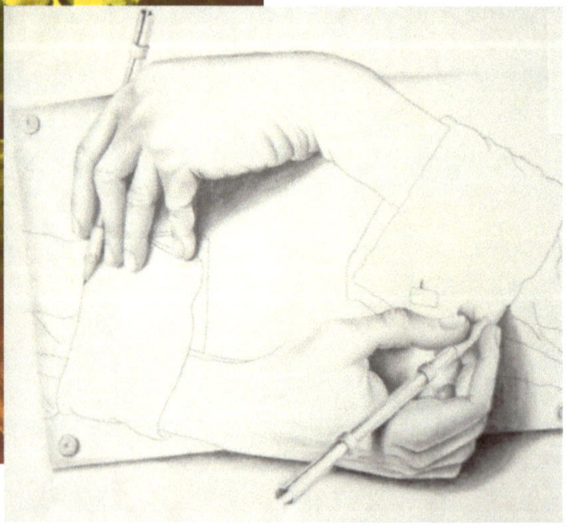

Ask a child to take a pencil in each hand and attempt to draw each wing of the eagle simultaneously by using both hands. "Try to do your best while using a pencil in the left hand for the left wing and pencil in the right hand for the right wing." See which of the drawings is more accurate.

If it is the left one, the child belongs to linguistic and creative category. If it is the right one, most likely he will be a scientist with a good reasoning.

Flamingo Family

Let's look on what makes the flamingo silhouette. It is curved lines. The painting is developed from negative (green color between head and neck and between neck and body) and positive spaces (flamingo head and body).

An artist has used different negative spaces to show the dynamic of the flamingo body. If an artist would draw the neck of the flamingo by vertical lines, not curved ones, the negative spaces would be changed as well. This change would make the painting boring, and the flamingo will not be as attractive as it is depicted on a painting. The child may try to change position of the neck and see what may happen.

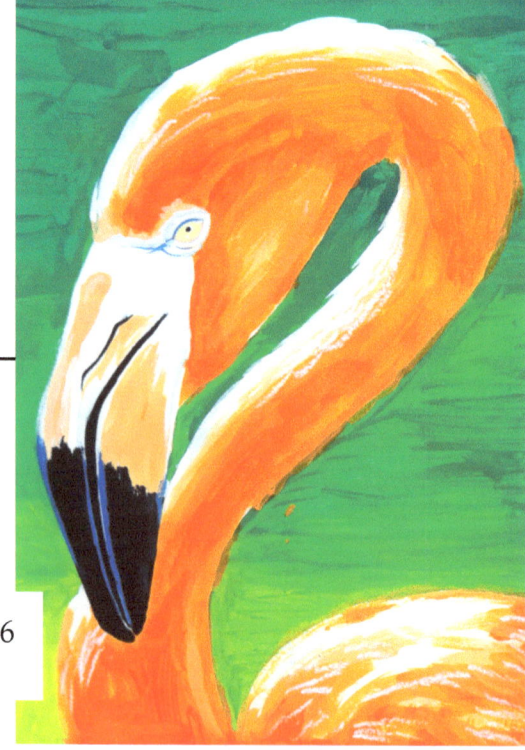

John Troshetti - age 6

On this page, you may join children in a forest when they play under autumn foliage. Bring an attention of a child to colorfulness and shapes of the leaves and propose him or her to draw at least some of them on the empty spot. Ask a child if he or she noticed that leaves have changed their size when they fall down.

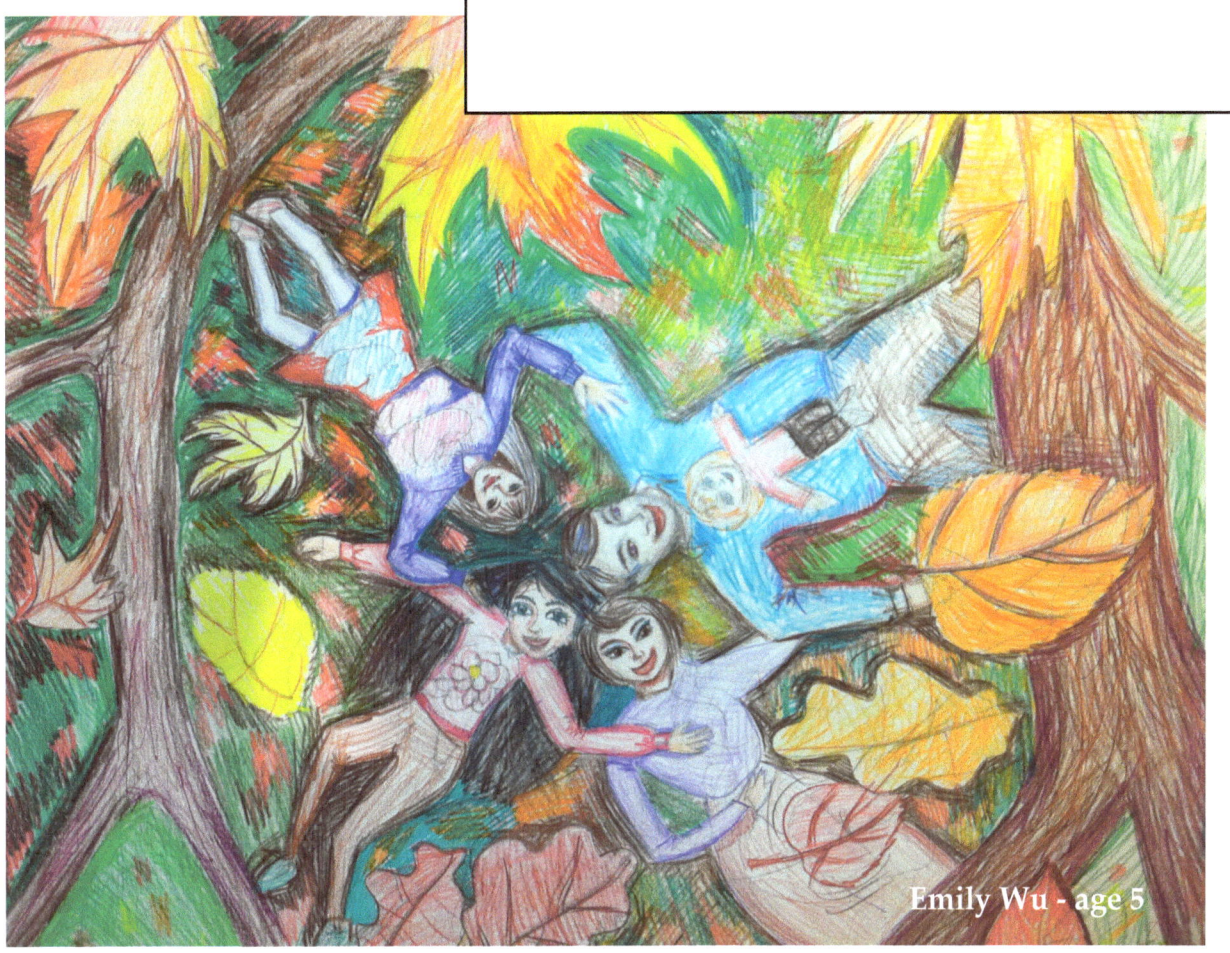

Emily Wu - age 5

Van Gouge Glass

This page is exceptional because it includes a copy of Van Gouge's famous painting Starring Night copied by a student. The curved strokes and bright opposite colors show mystery of the night and a quick change of life.

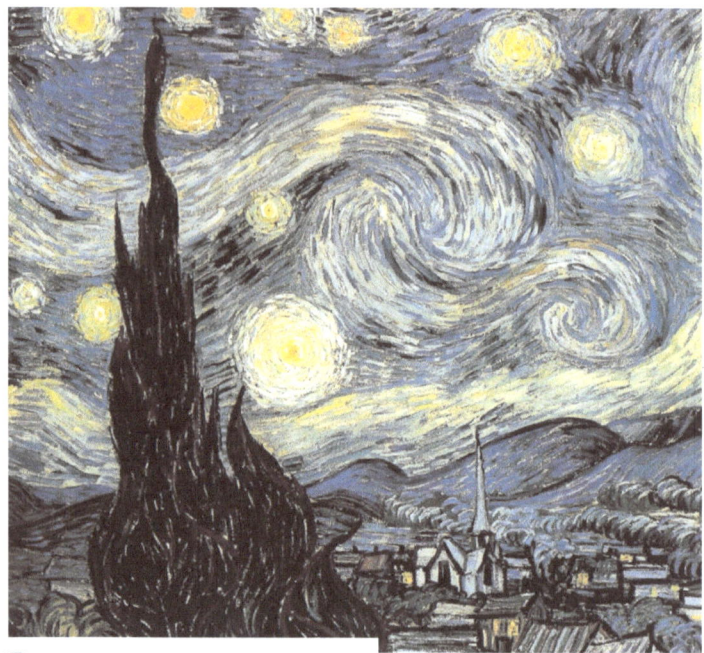

Adult Student

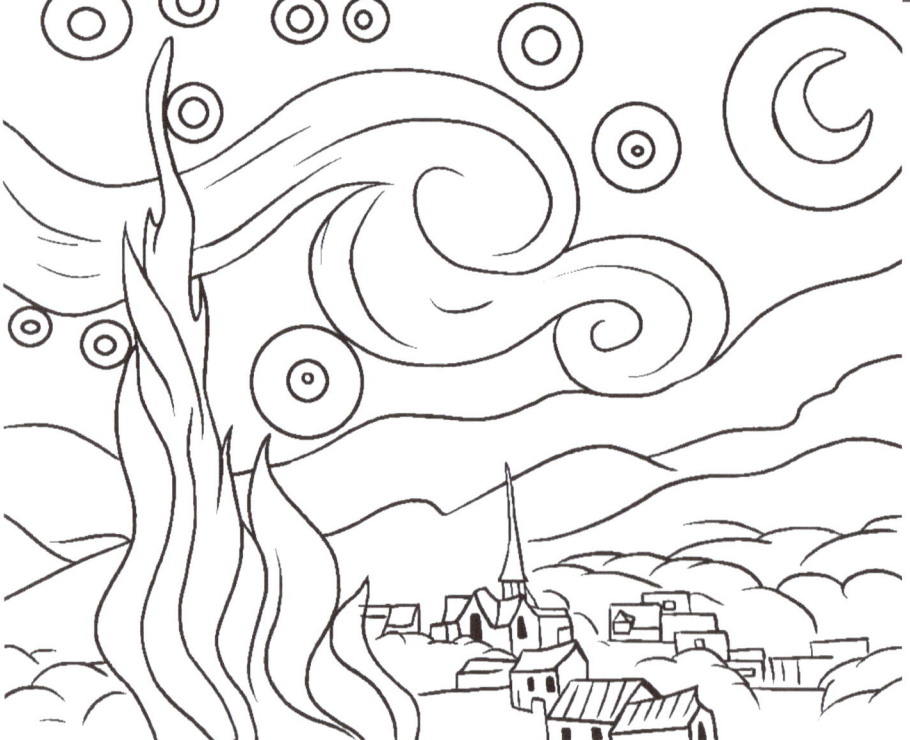

A notLASSpainting includes a variety of **GLASS** bottles and vases. A bright-striped background has been seen through each glass item differently.

Try to find at home some empty bottles of different colors or different thickness, put them upfront of any colorful background. You may use color paper as a background. Ask a child to look at the background through the different glass items. Find out why the background is seen very well through some of the bottles and why the background is seen just partially through other bottles. Be careful with the glass.

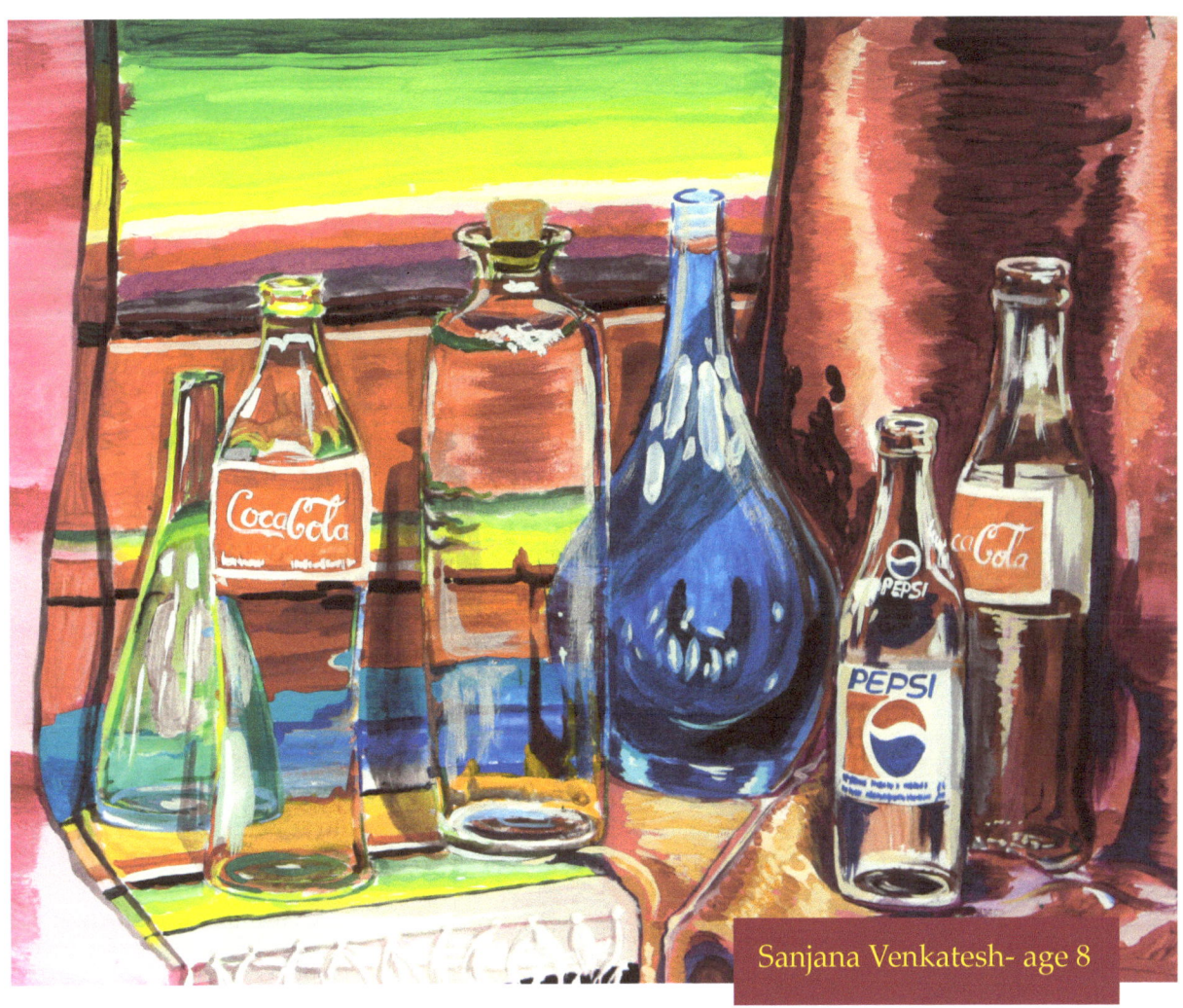

Sanjana Venkatesh- age 8

Halloween Harvest

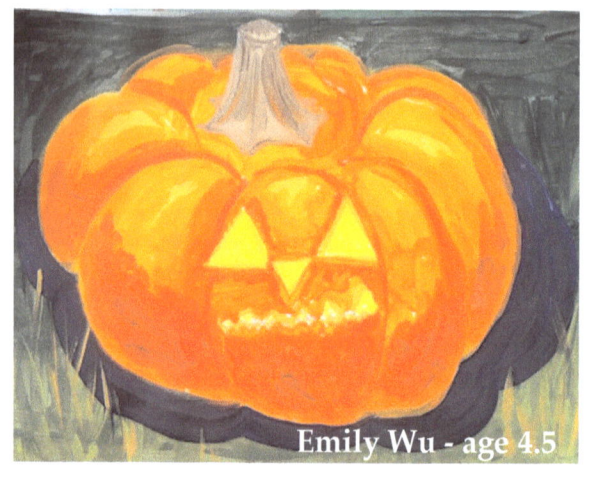

Emily Wu - age 4.5

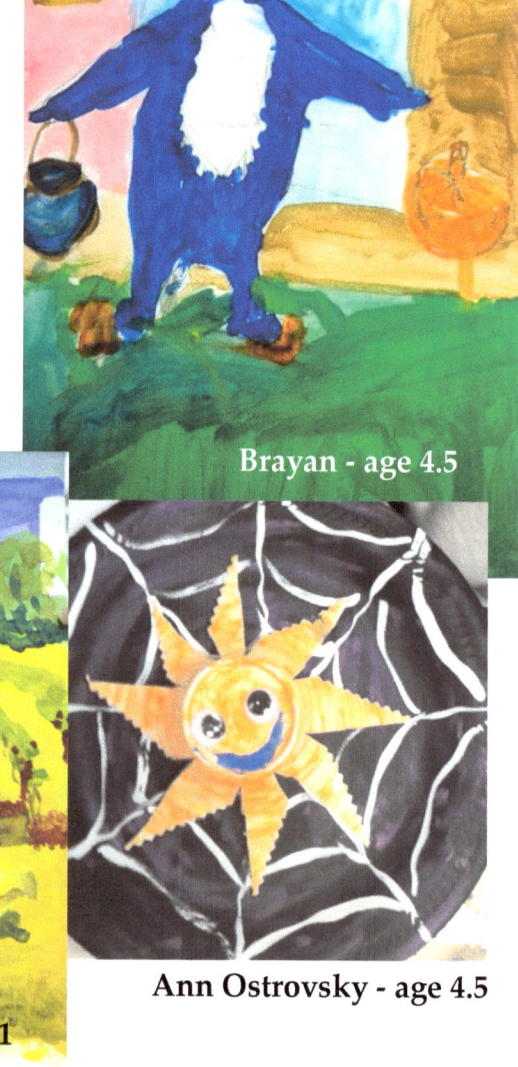

Brayan - age 4.5

Emily - age 11

Ann Ostrovsky - age 4.5

Three paintings on «H» page reflect *Halloween* items and actions. The forth painting depicts *harvest*. What connections do all these paintings have? What was taken from the basket on a painting representing harvest and used in a painting, representing Halloween? Ask a child to draw and paint this item on this empty spot. What shape would make this item smiling?

Illustration

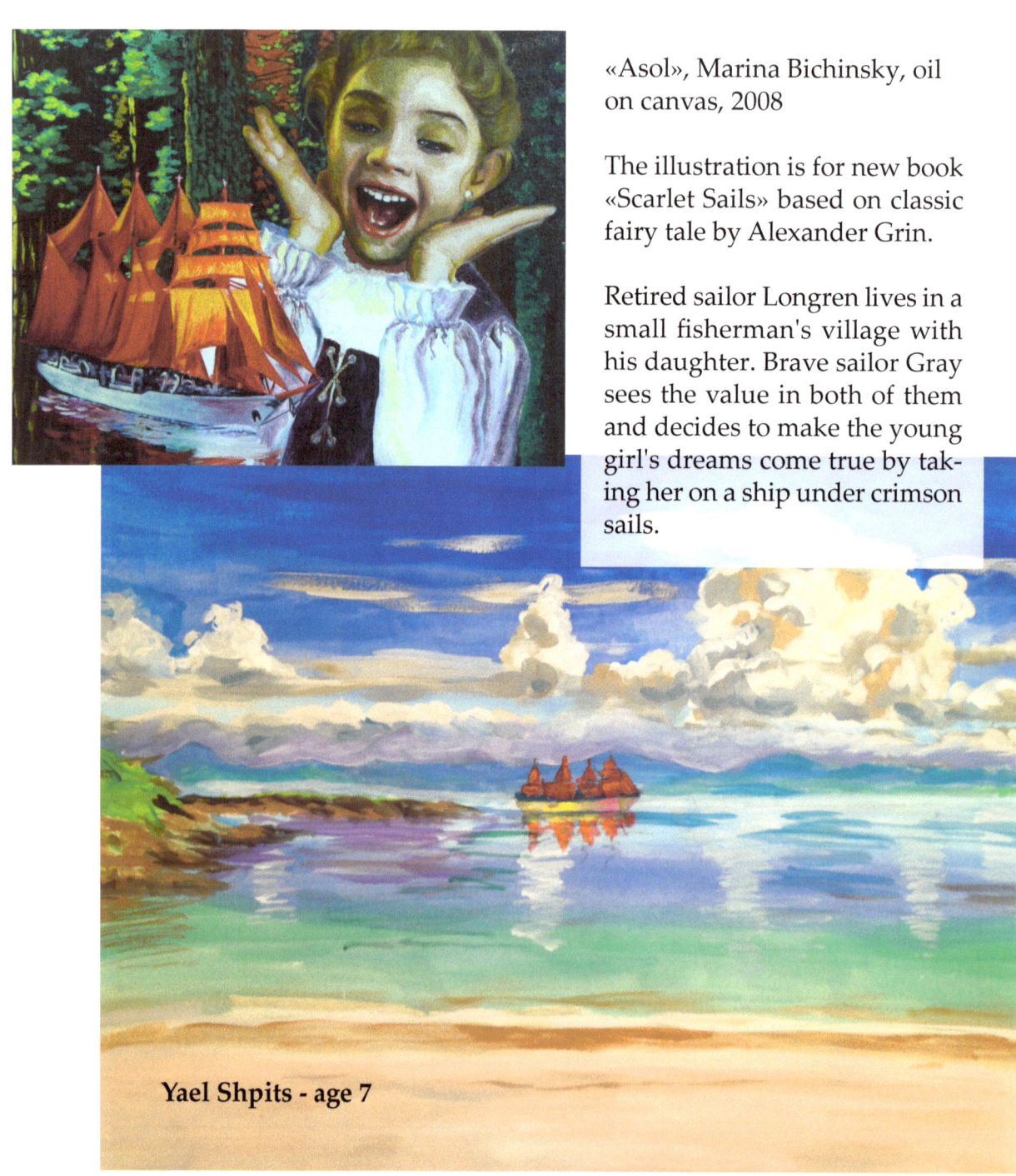

«Asol», Marina Bichinsky, oil on canvas, 2008

The illustration is for new book «Scarlet Sails» based on classic fairy tale by Alexander Grin.

Retired sailor Longren lives in a small fisherman's village with his daughter. Brave sailor Gray sees the value in both of them and decides to make the young girl's dreams come true by taking her on a ship under crimson sails.

Yael Shpits - age 7

An Illustration is a picture that may tell a story without text or support of written words. If a child did not see a ship with scarlet sails before, he may find how it looks like in the illustrations by Marina Bichinsky on the top and the young artist on the bottom of the page. The child also may be not familiar with the word "excitement." Thus the illustration on the top will introduce him or her to this feeling, reflected on the girl's face. May your child understand what the word reflection of the ship in a water means? If not, the illustration will show what it means. Ask your child what would he or she add to the illustration that the young artist did to make a story about Asol clearer? Would your child bring Asol, her father, or the prince together? Draw the background on empty spot bellow. Then a child may draw all personages on a separate paper, cut them out and then place them on the background of the illustration and make a "Scarlet Sails" play.

Jacket
Jar

Ankita Akerkar -
age 15 -->

Adult Student

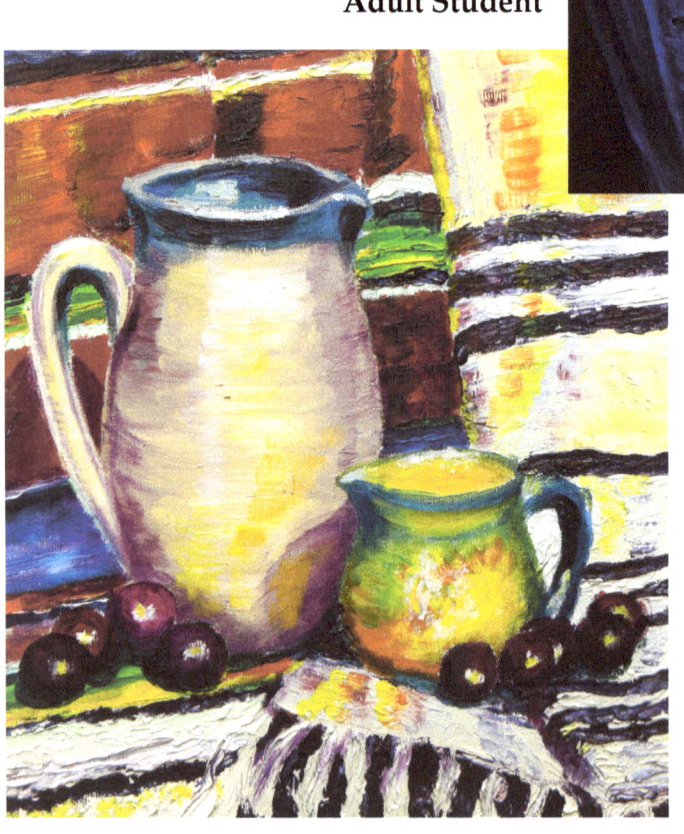

The top painting reflects the leather jacket hanging on a chair and another painting depicts two jars. Both paintings are called a **still life** because they reproduce unmoved subjects. Both paintings include many details and a variety of small and big items. For instance, the leather jacket consists of the collar, pockets, zips, and buttons. Young artist used a variety colors to show leather's shining surface.

Capability to see the details on paintings is one of the most important key ingredients that provide the opportunity to read the story beyond the illustration or a "genre" painting. Could your child see that the artist depicted a small theatrical purse inside of the jacket? Indeed. Could the purse provoke a child's imagination that it is an evening gown or a dress for the ballerina? This is the one story. What may happen with the story if instead of purse artist would depict an envelope?

This small element is very important because a child may become a co-author of the story while deciding who wrote the letter and to whom. Inserting a letter in the jacket, young artist knows that this letter is very important and should be sent as soon as possible. Dramatic color of the background supports this assumption. What is in the letter? A child may decide.

Ask a child to draw illustration representing context of the letter.

Kayak
Keys

The photo-realistic painting below was created by using acrylic paint. The artist was very oriented to details and used multi-layering technique to show bright subjects against the dark background. Please take attention of the child to shadows and half tones of the lock that make subject rounded on a site. To reach the quality of such type of painting, a child needs to develop his or her skills during a few years.

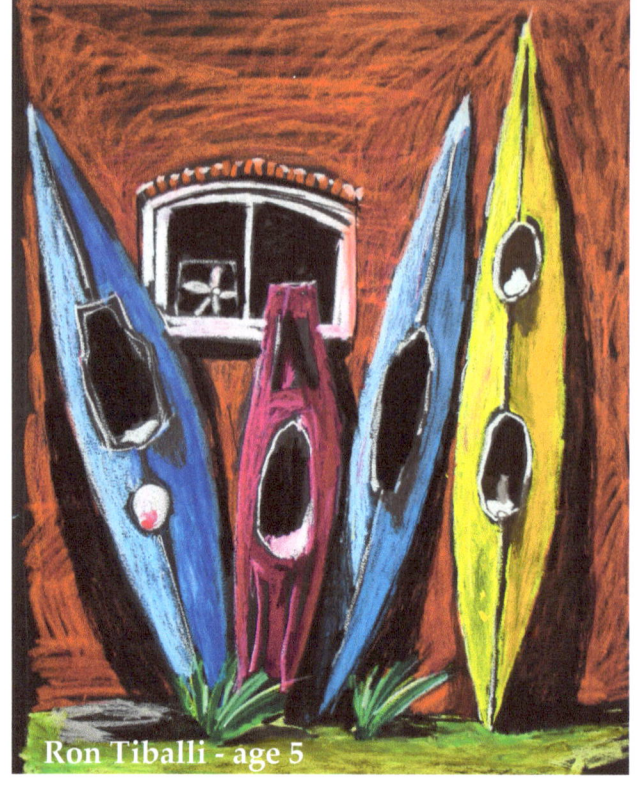

Ron Tiballi - age 5

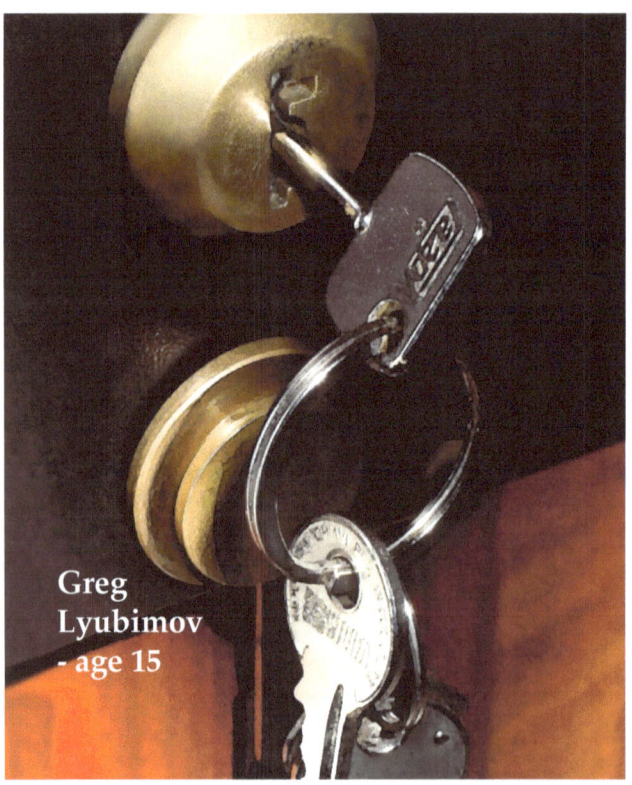

Greg Lyubimov - age 15

This young artist used the pastel sticks to draw a few kayaks. He puts the kayaks to dry on the red wall. Working on a dark-colored paper, the artist leaved a black shadow from the kayaks on the wall to create illusion of a warm sunny day. The surface of each boat was depicted by the light and dark shade of blue, red, and yellow to show that the surface is constructed by two equal parts. Ask a child to master his or her own kayak and paint it in this technique, which is quite similar to coloring the subjects by color pencils.

Landscape

Landscape art is the depiction of natural scenery such as mountains, valleys, gardens, beaches, and forests. Artists use this type of art when they want to show a panoramic view or a big picture of the particular scenery. Landscape art is also used by artists as a background for historical or contemporary events with figurine compositions. The sky on a painting develops the mood. For instance, the rainbows on the sky on the painting on the left represent a happy day among beautiful valley. Please ask a child to determine the role the sky plays on other compositions presented on the right.

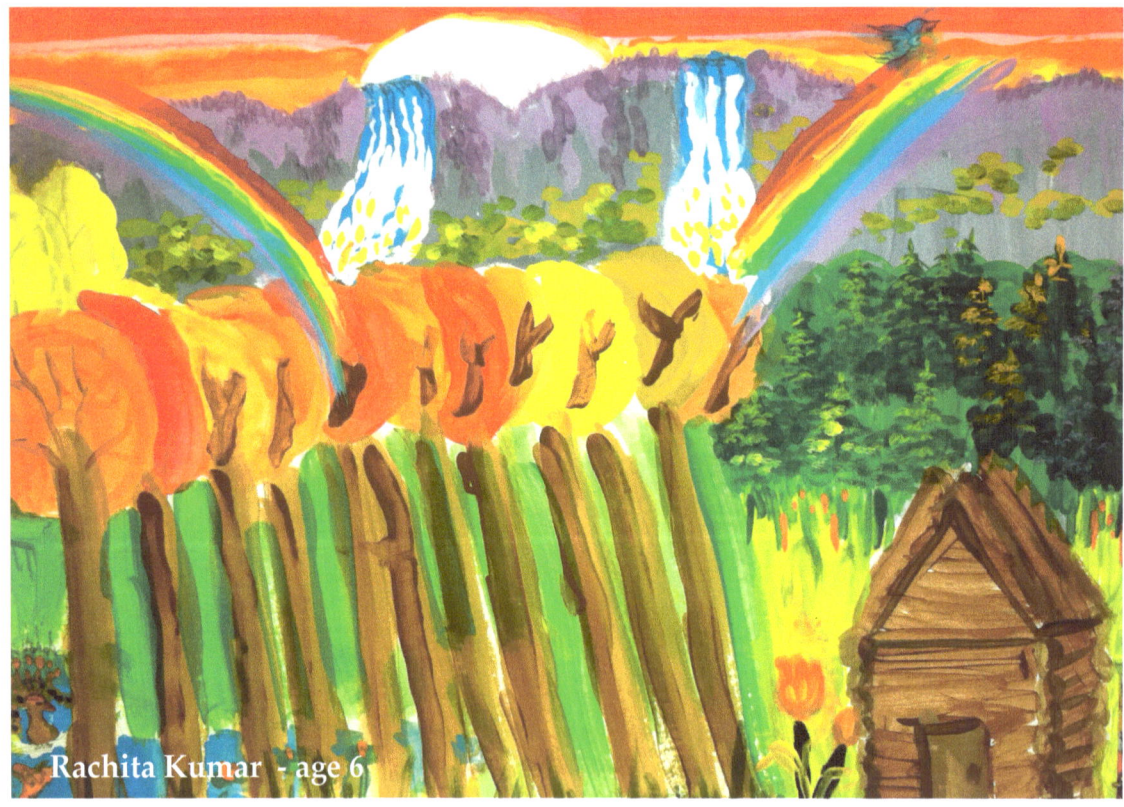

Rachita Kumar - age 6

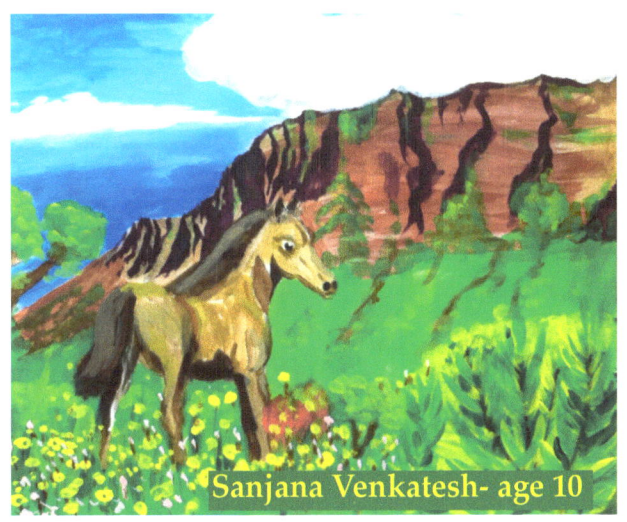

Sanjana Venkatesh- age 10

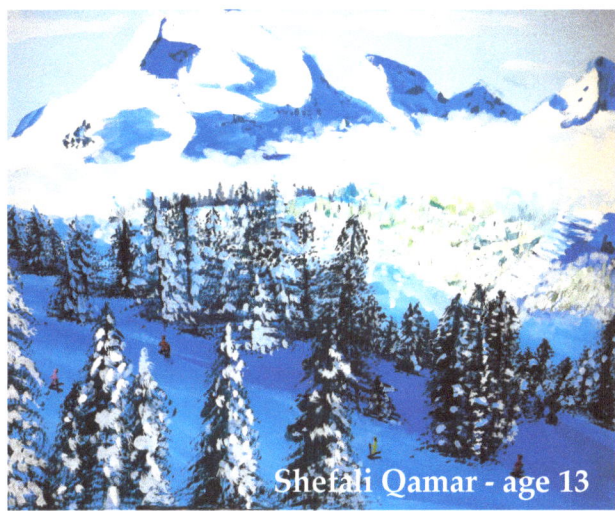

Shefali Qamar - age 13

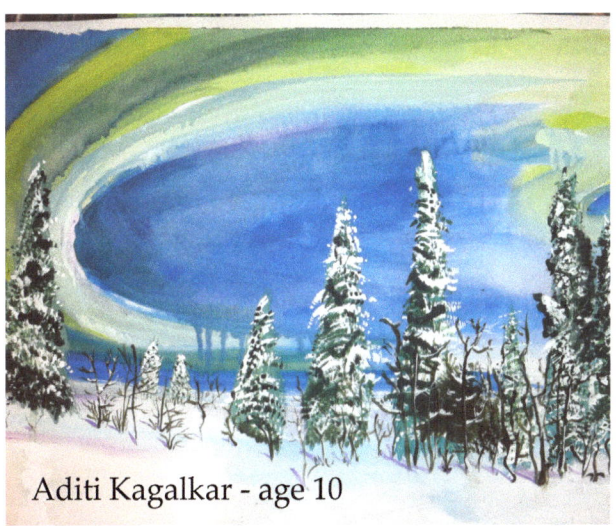

Aditi Kagalkar - age 10

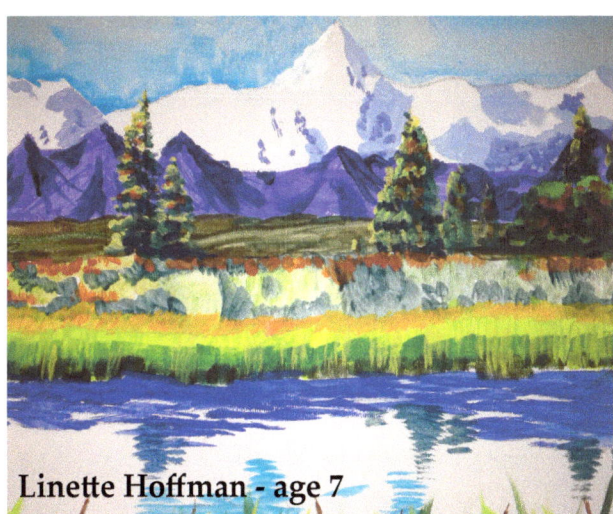

Linette Hoffman - age 7

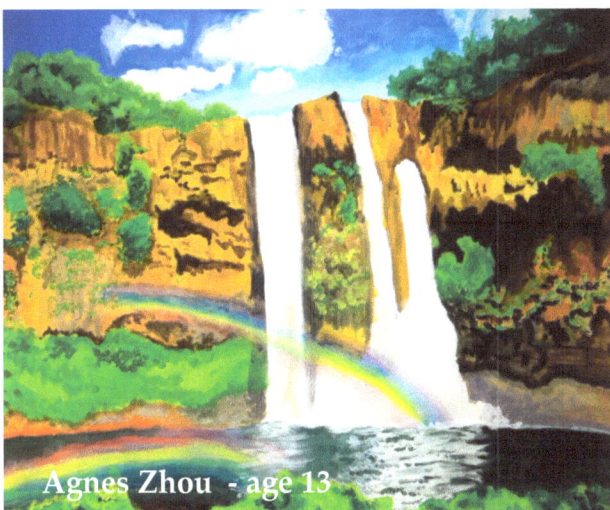

Agnes Zhou - age 13

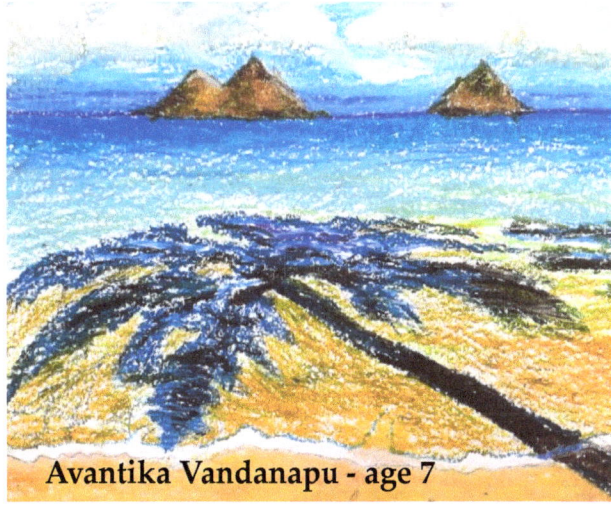

Avantika Vandanapu - age 7

Monet
Mario
Mosquito

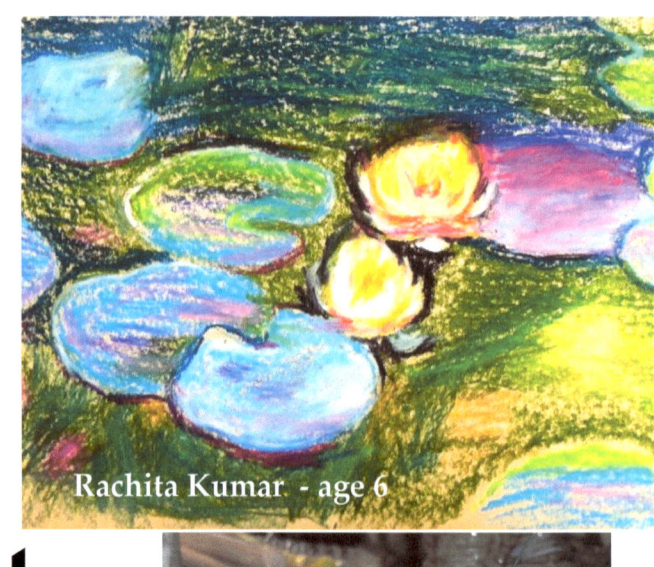

Rachita Kumar - age 6

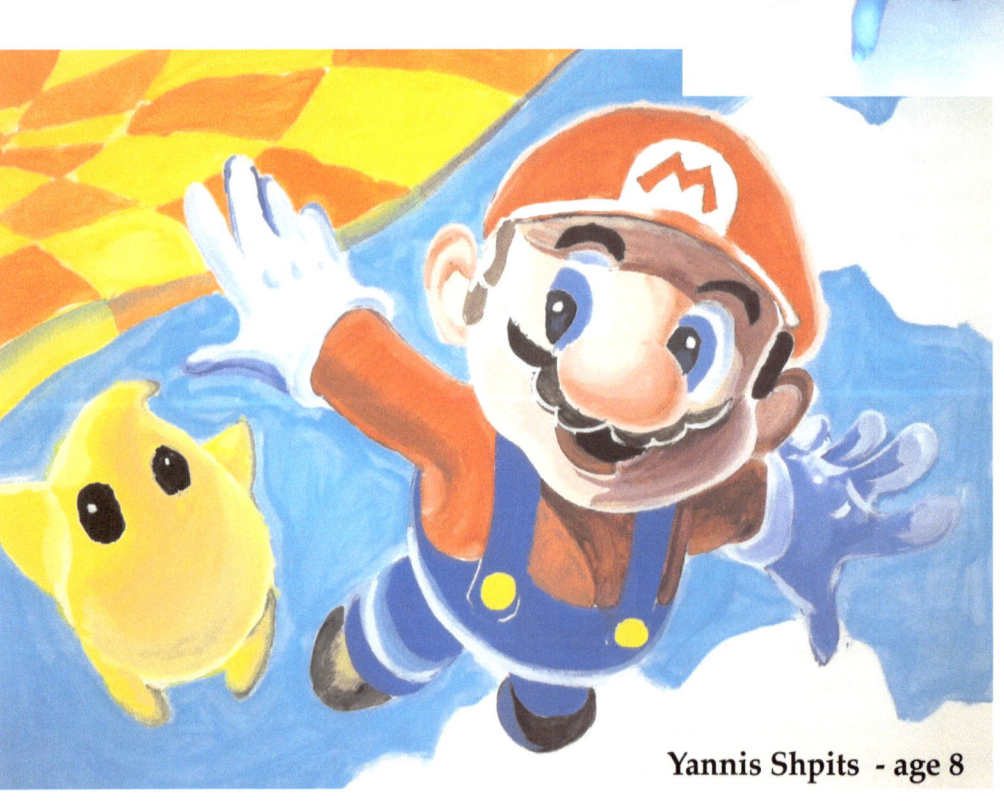

Yannis Shpits - age 8

The paintings for the letter «M» include a copy of Monet's painting (fragment-part), an illustration from the "Mario Brothers" Wii game cover, and a sculpture of a Mosquito.

The artist depicted the pond has used oil pastel. Illustration on the game cover was painted by acrylic, and the mosquito was created by clay. Different painting techniques produce different views on a work.

Let a child decide which work includes a cartoon character and which one is done in impressionistic manner. Impressionist depicts images along with reflections from other subjects and such surrounding as sky, earth, or water. Caricaturist presents his or her image symbolically while highlighting the major characteristics in a funny manner.

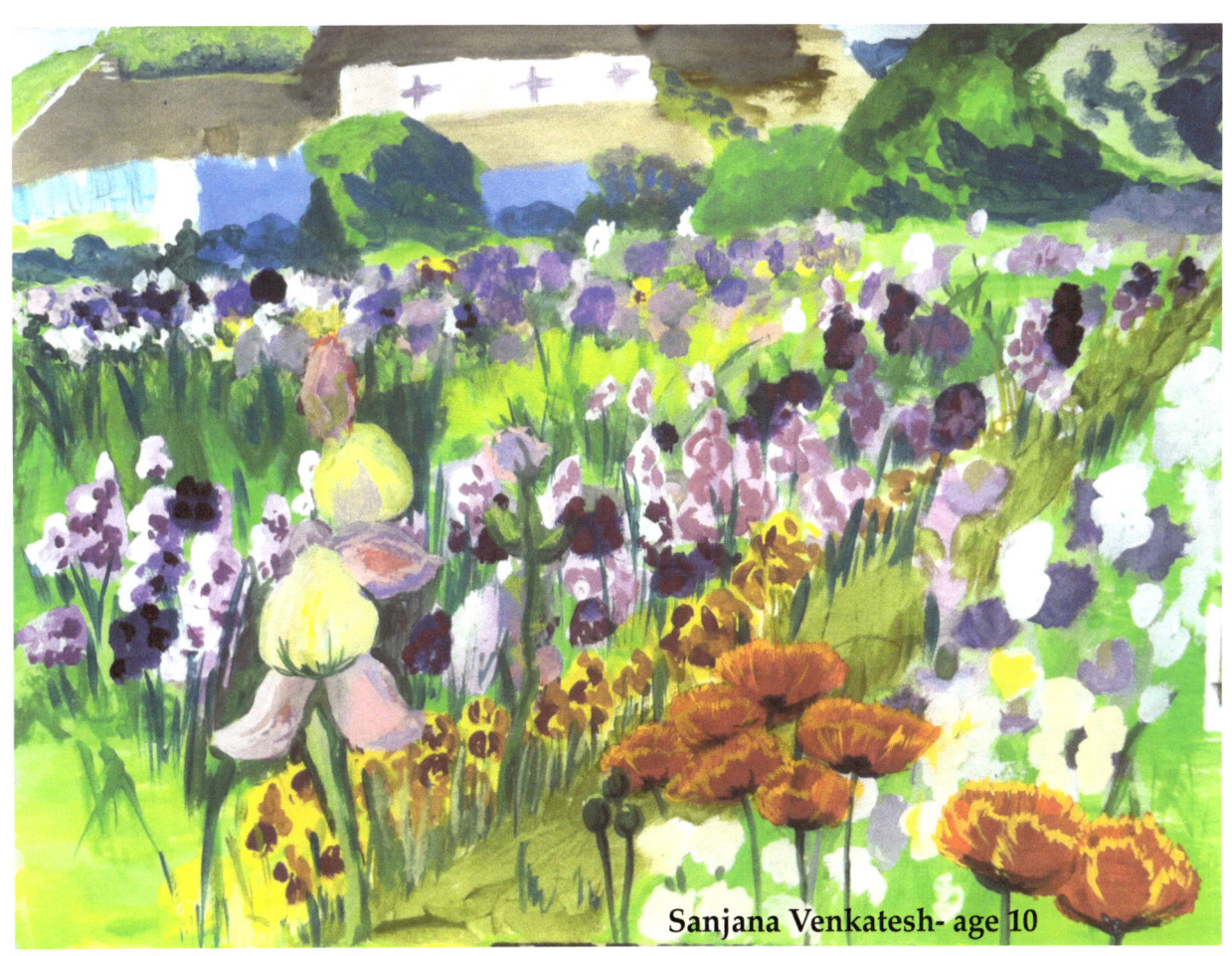

Sanjana Venkatesh- age 10

Night
Nemo

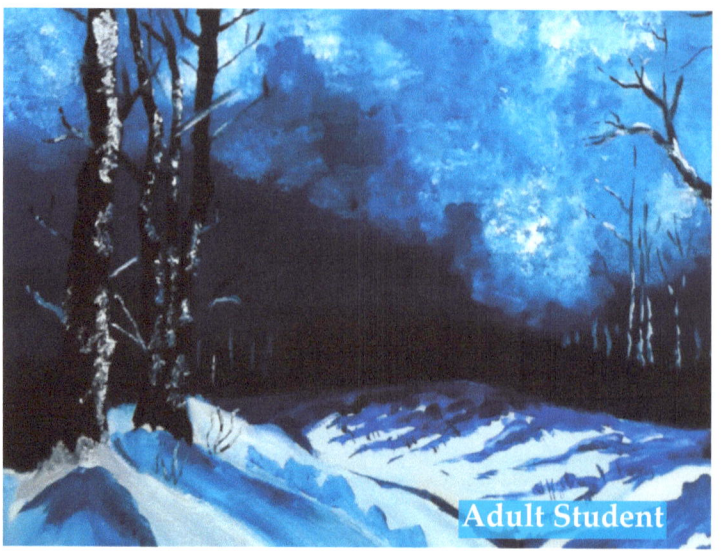

Adult Student

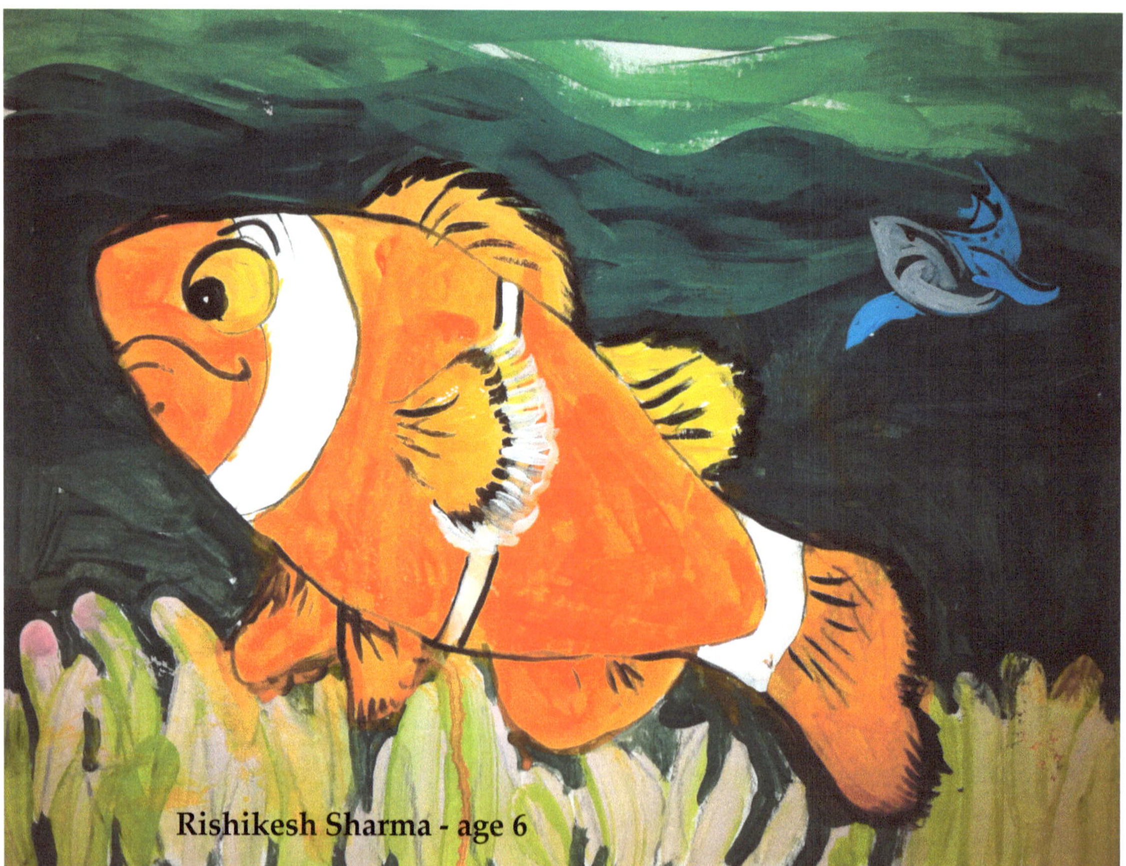

Rishikesh Sharma - age 6

Could your child recognize the letter "L" on the painting representing Night. It is the «L» composition, in which the shadow on the snow laid down from the trees. In this composition, depiction of snow includes many details, which would disappear in a distance. Ask a child to find similarity and differences within the ends of the curved lines. A child may try to repeat them while making drawings on separate paper.

Orange

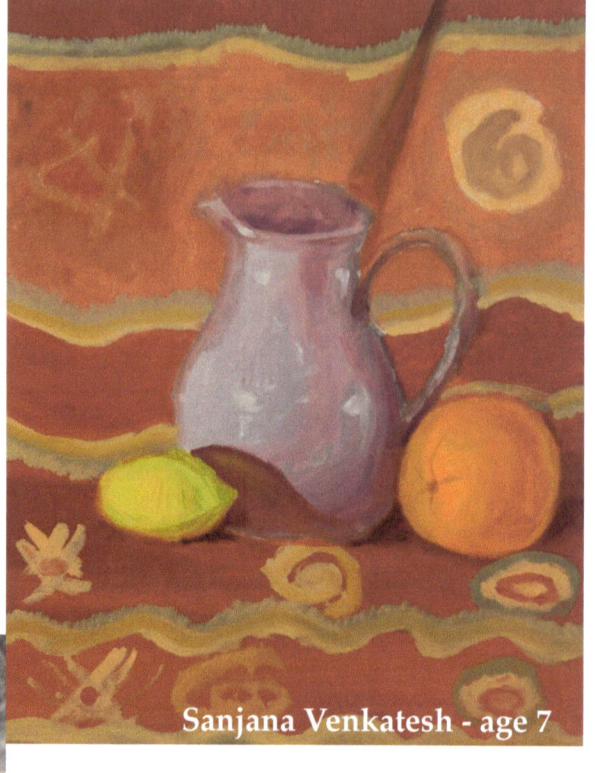

Sanjana Venkatesh - age 7

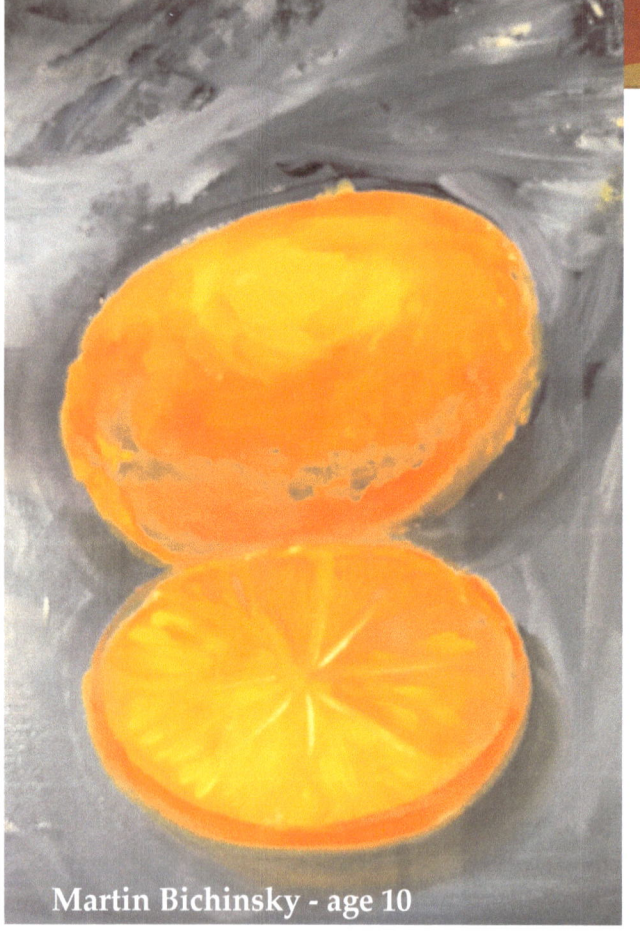

Martin Bichinsky - age 10

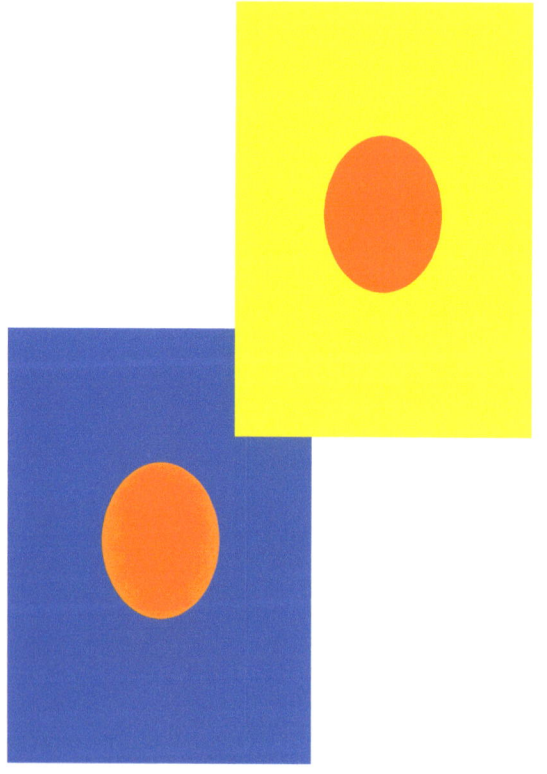

The paintings on both pictures include an orange. On the left painting, the orange is brighter than the orange on the right one. Ask a child to find out why. What color made the orange on the left more shining? Artist has used this color to depict the lemon on the right painting, but the orange on the left painting still looks brighter. Perhaps artist added or mixed this color with the white or another kind of yellow. Please note that any object depicted on the dark background will look brighter. Ask a child to make this bright color below.

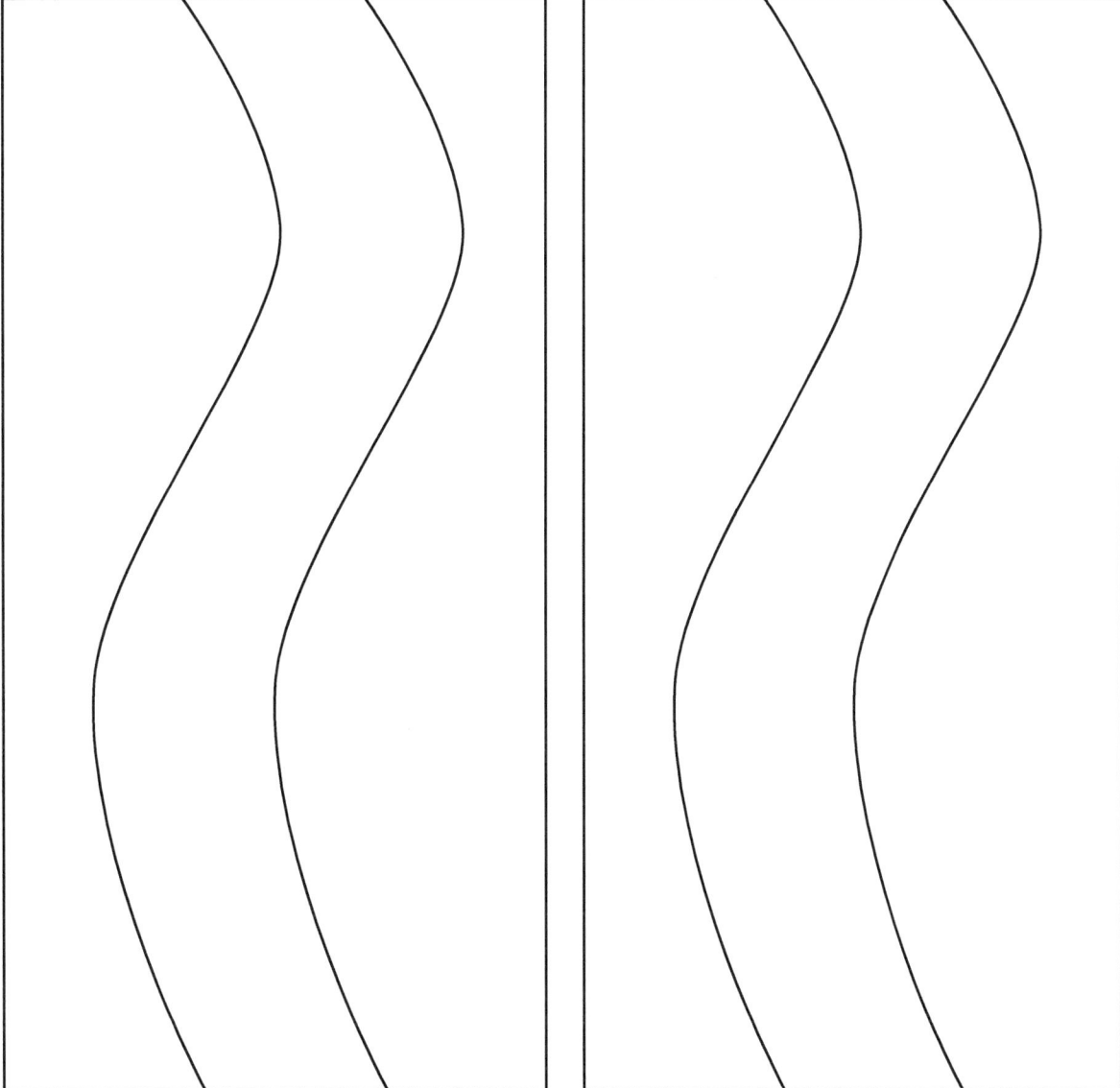

Pear

Pinguin

Pizza

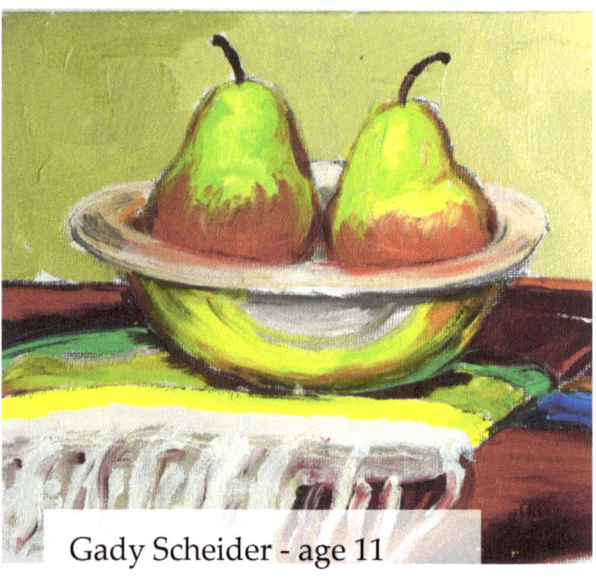

Gady Scheider - age 11

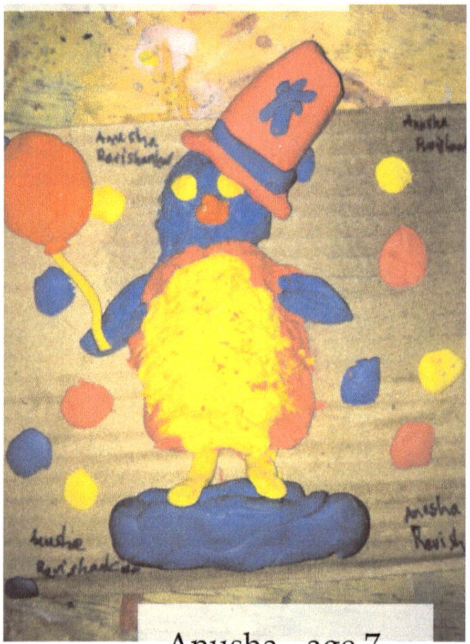

Anusha - age 7

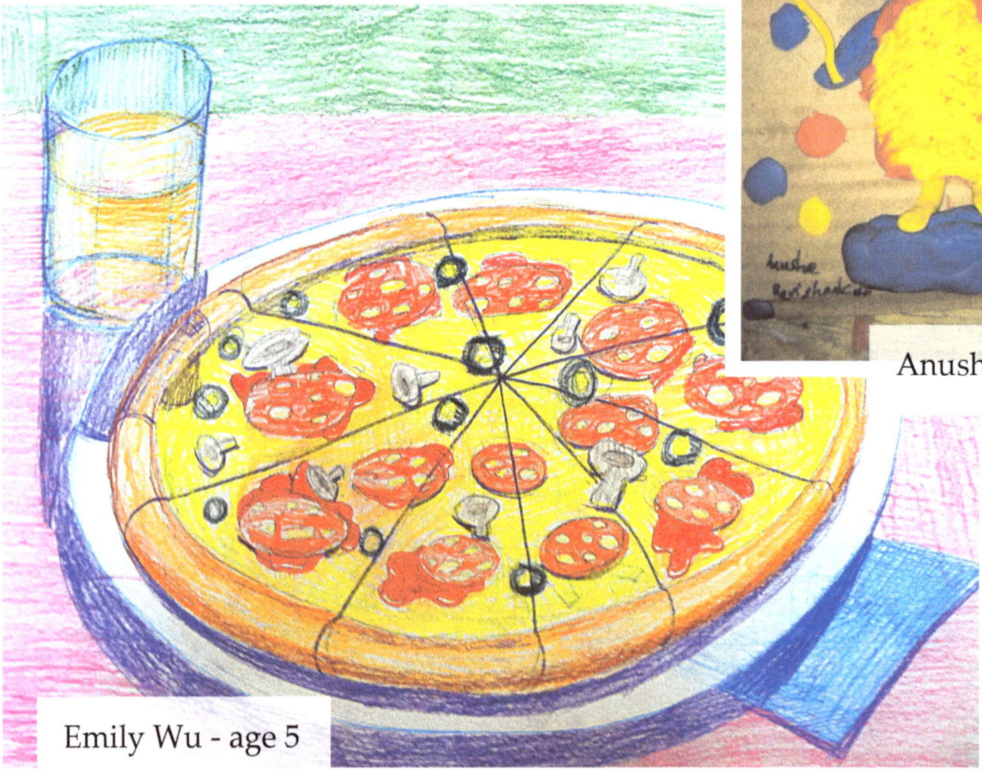

Emily Wu - age 5

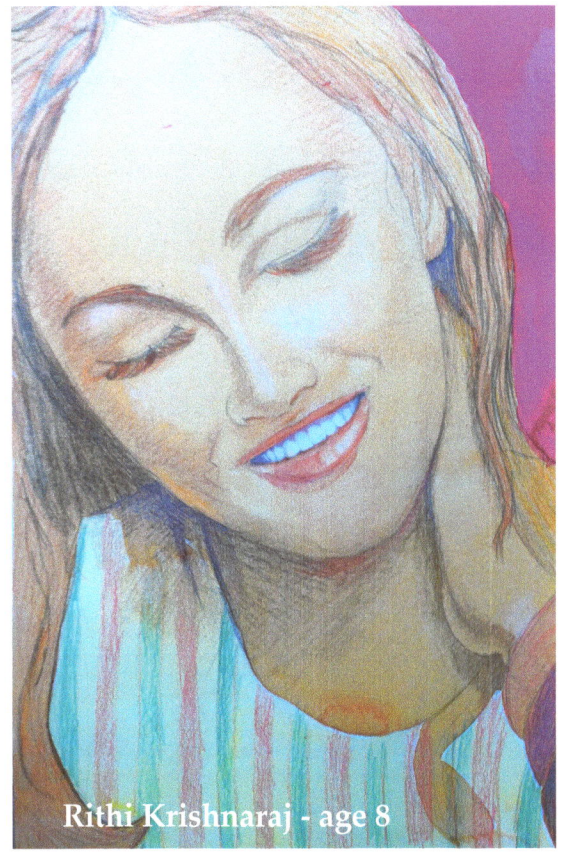

Rithi Krishnaraj - age 8

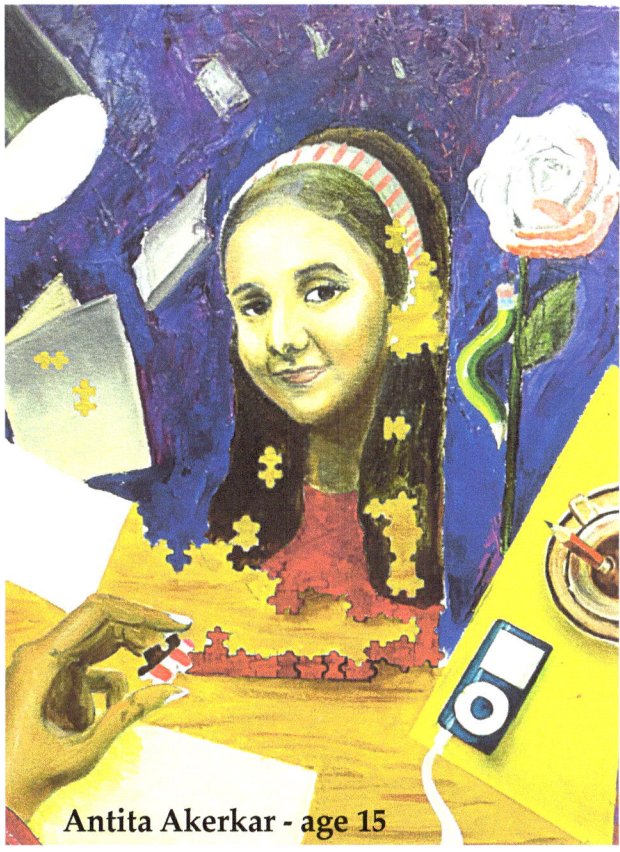

Antita Akerkar - age 15

Pizza, Penguin, and Pears are presented here for letter «P». What is common for all these paintings? Pizza is divided by triangular slices; both pears are depicted by triangular shapes. The top of the bowl with the pears is created by two ovals; shapes of the plate with pizza are also created by two ovals. The penguin's body is also created by two ovals.

What about the letter «P» for these two PORTRAITS? The self portrait on the right represents a SURREALISM, which means that artist used collage to surprise a viewer and provide her interpretation of what is depicted. Let's try to understand how the artist wanted to introduce herself when she approached her 16th birthday. This high-school student did not know about herself enough to say the story. So she depicted herself as a non-complete puzzle. On the left lower corner of the picture we can see the artist's hand building the puzzle. Ask a child what he or she would include in his or her self-portrait.

Queen

A princess will become a queen when she would stop caring about only her dresses and will start worrying about the people in her kingdom.

She also would need to learn not only good manners and people skills but also to understand what to do to make a peaceful and happy life for all.

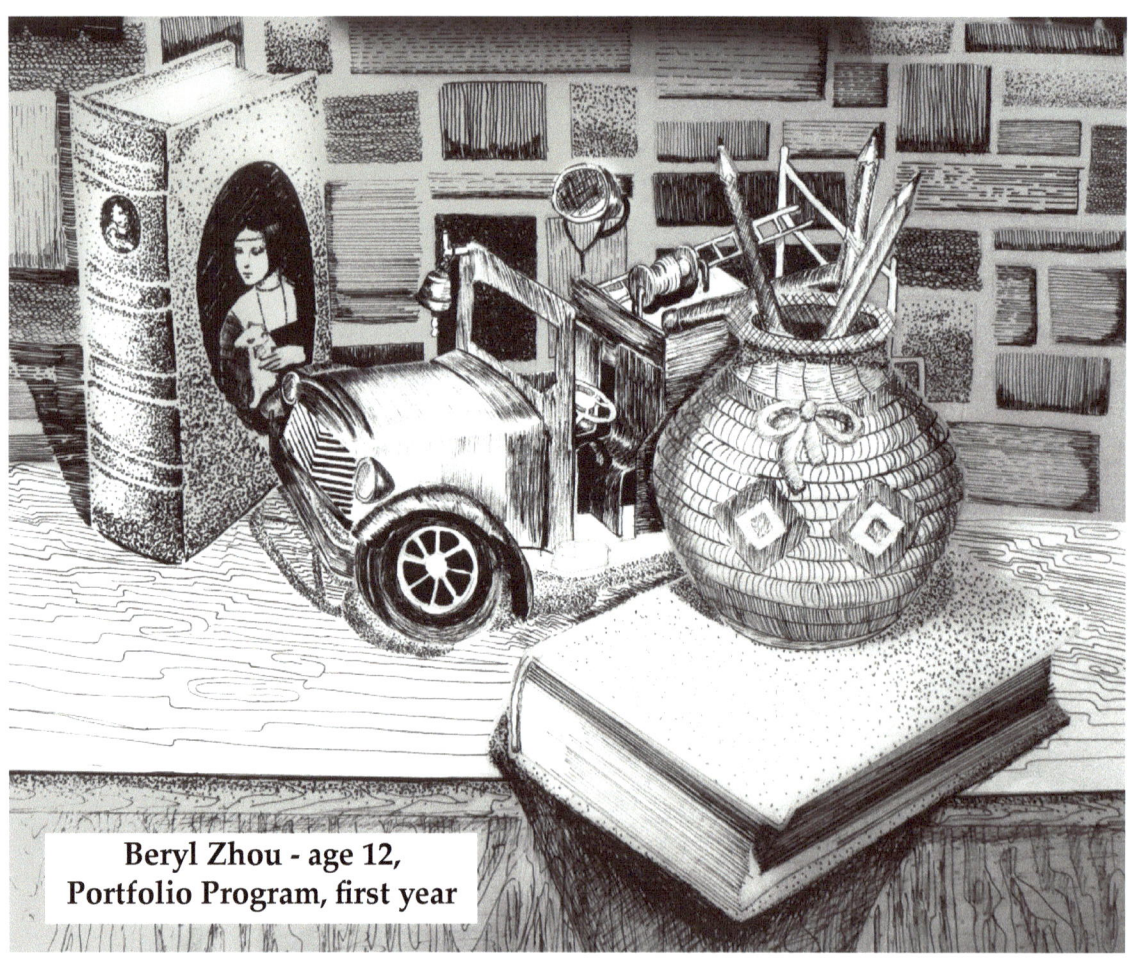

Beryl Zhou - age 12,
Portfolio Program, first year

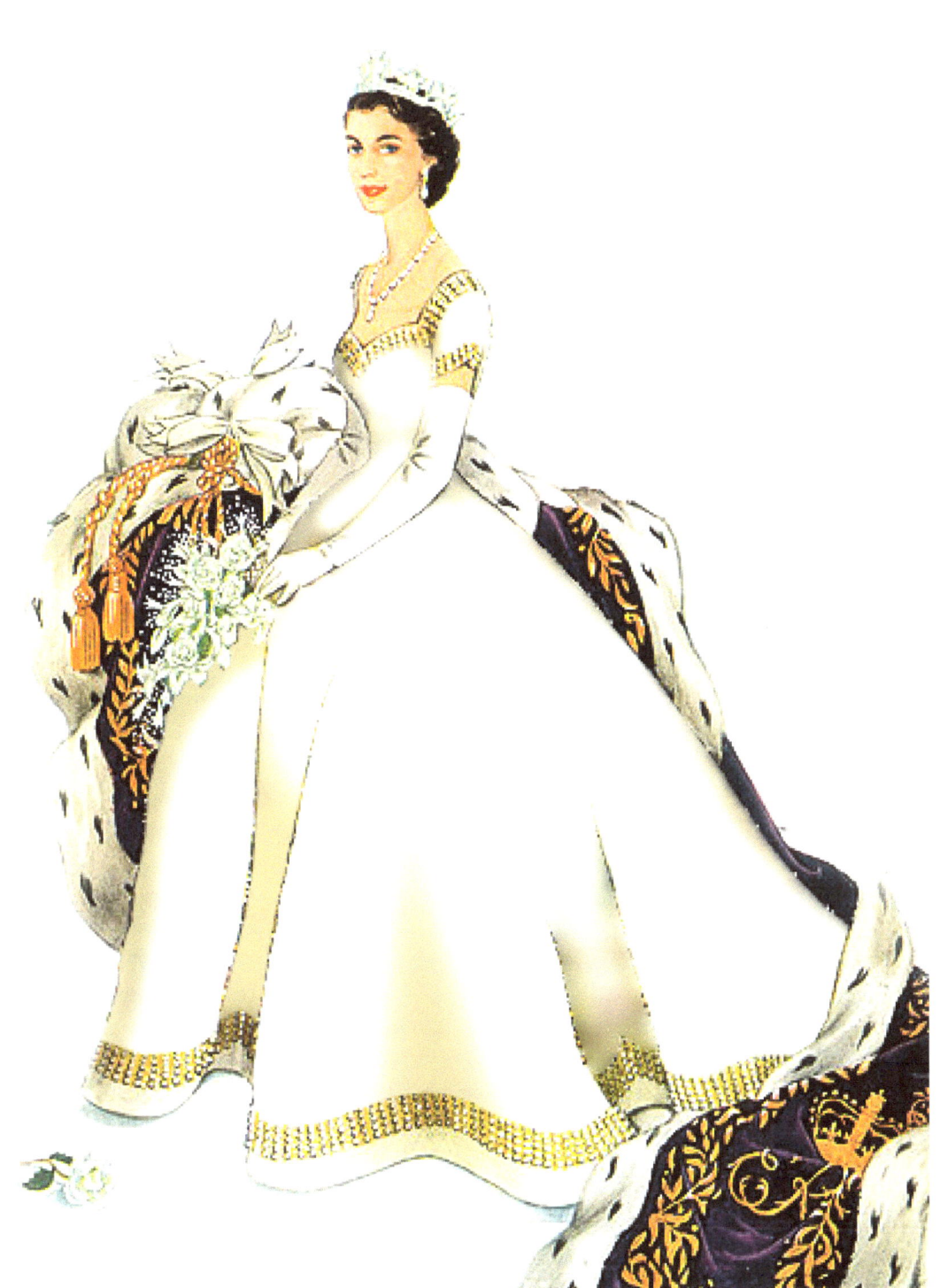

Rooster
Rainbow
Rubens

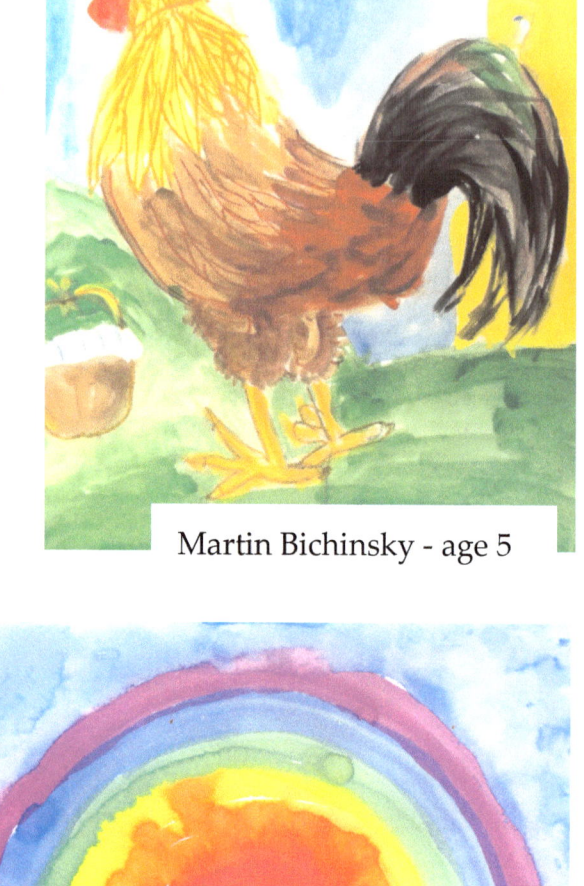

Martin Bichinsky - age 5

Adult Student

Martin Bichinsky - age 3

The student's copy of the Portrait of a Boy by Paul Peter Rubens is included on a page along with paintings of the Rooster and the Rainbow. Why a boy's portrait has shown along with the symbols of the morning (Rooster) and freshness (Rainbow)? The portrait of a boy by Rubens is also a symbol of new life that connected to freshness and morning of the life. Moreover, the artist's last name begins with «R». Ask a child to make a story by using these three elements.

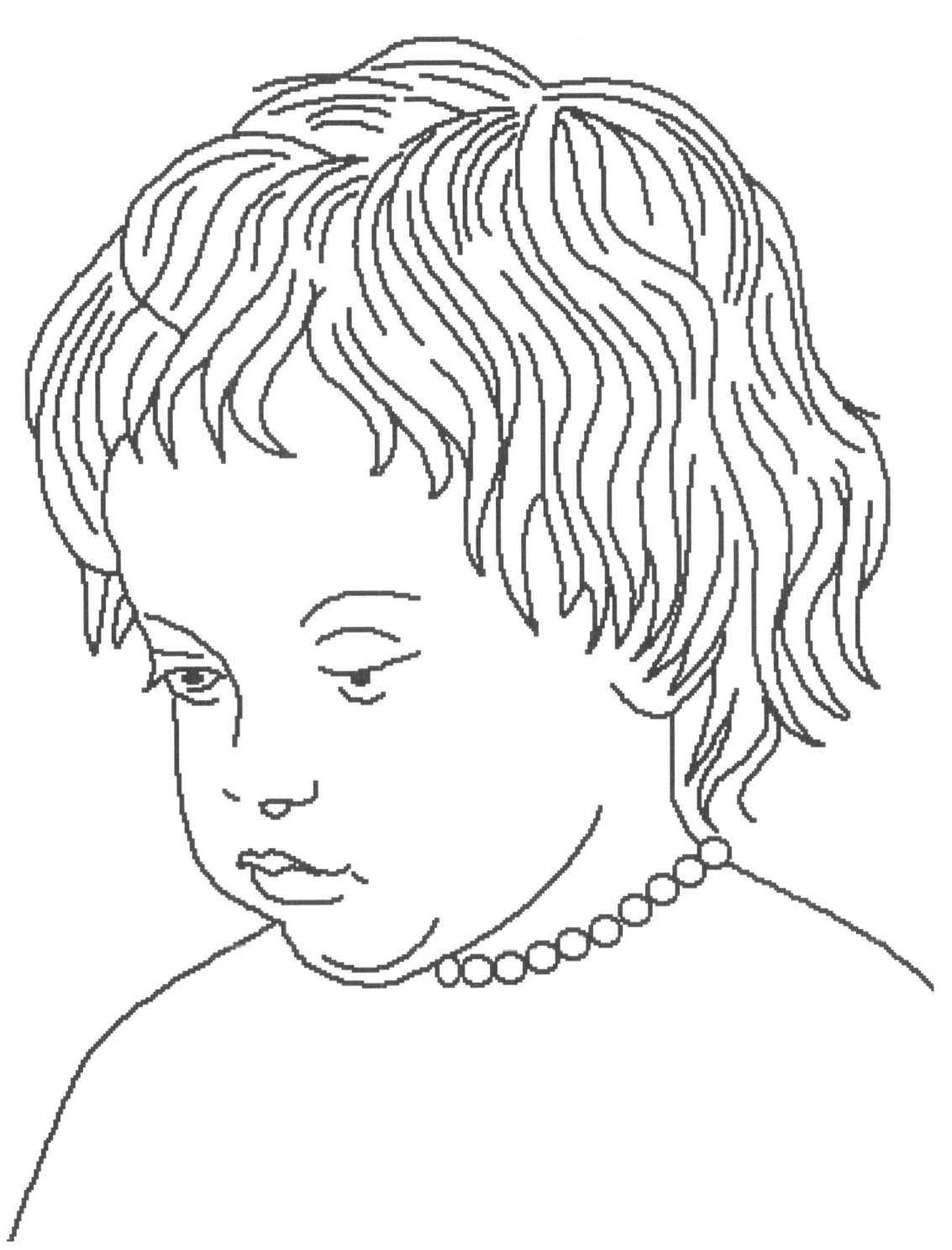

Still life

A still life is a work of art depicting compositions consisted floral, seascape, or timeless subjects such as flowers, exotic fruits, birds, rocks, books, glasses, watches, or candles. One of the purposes of these paintings is to decorate living rooms, while other purposes are to show people that life is beautiful by short. Still life in religious and historical paintings plays role of indicating era when a particular event took place.

The young artist used this style to represent subjects, surrounding him in his childhood, which would remind him later in a life about his favorite Teddy Bear and Tea party he had with his friends.

Please ask a child about his favorite toys and dishes? Does he or she like ice-cream, and with which flavor?

Could he draw a scoop in an ice-cream cone? What about sprinkles?

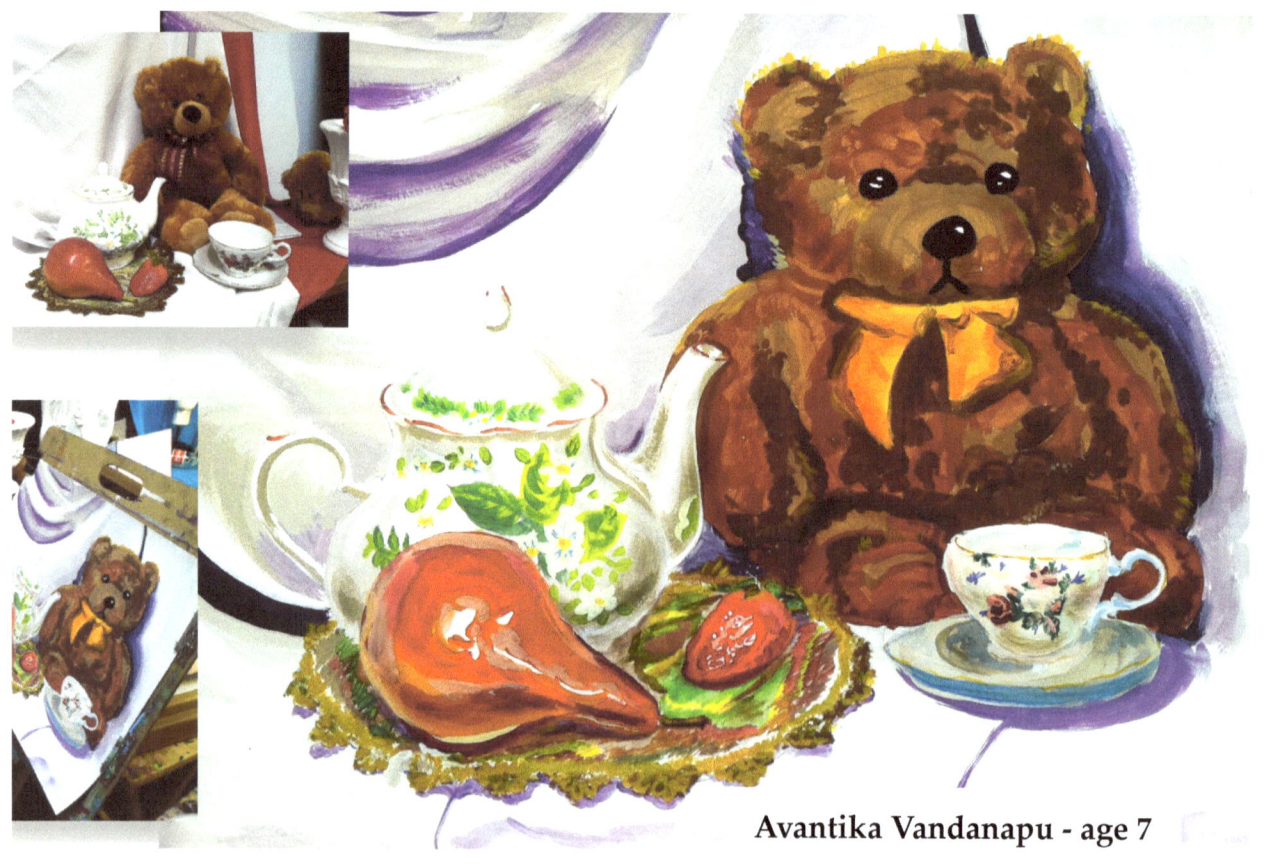

Avantika Vandanapu - age 7

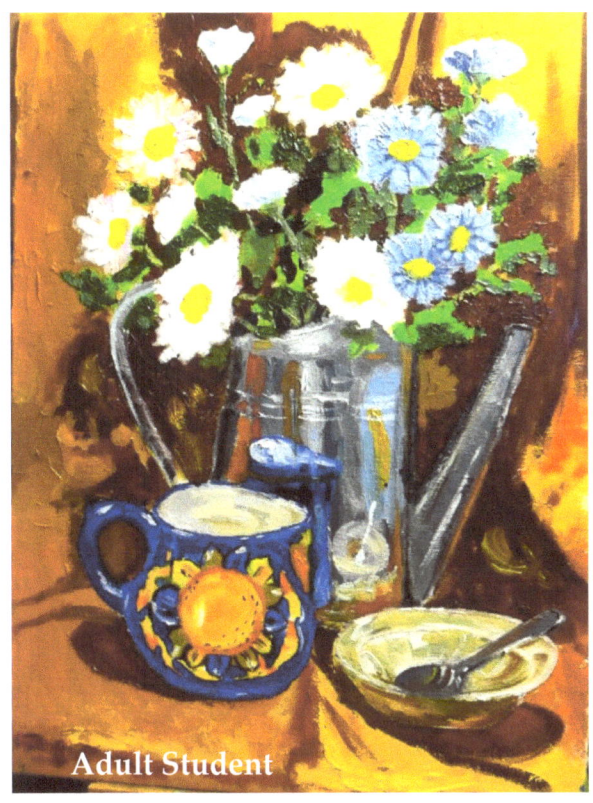

Adult Student

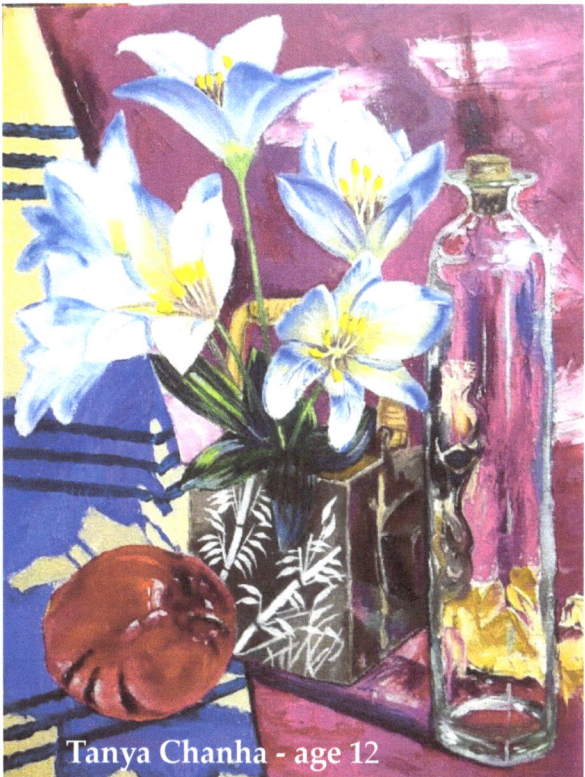

Tanya Chanha - age 12

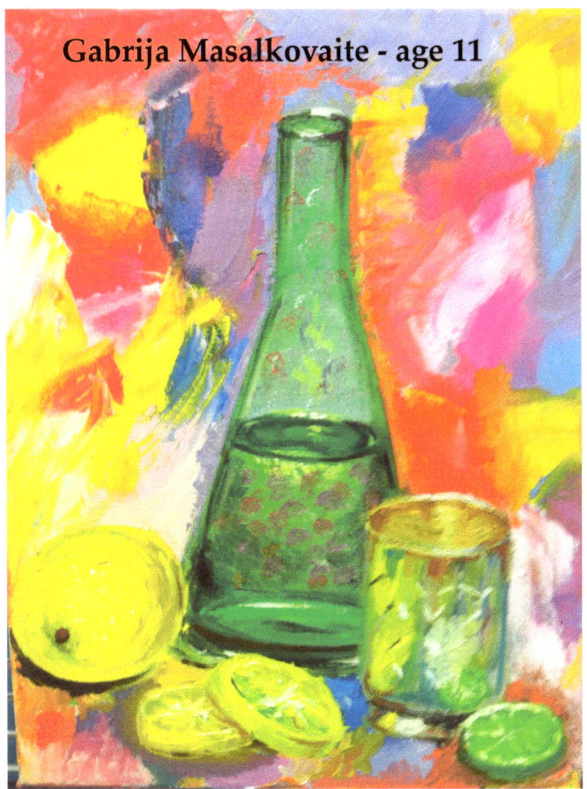

Gabrija Masalkovaite - age 11

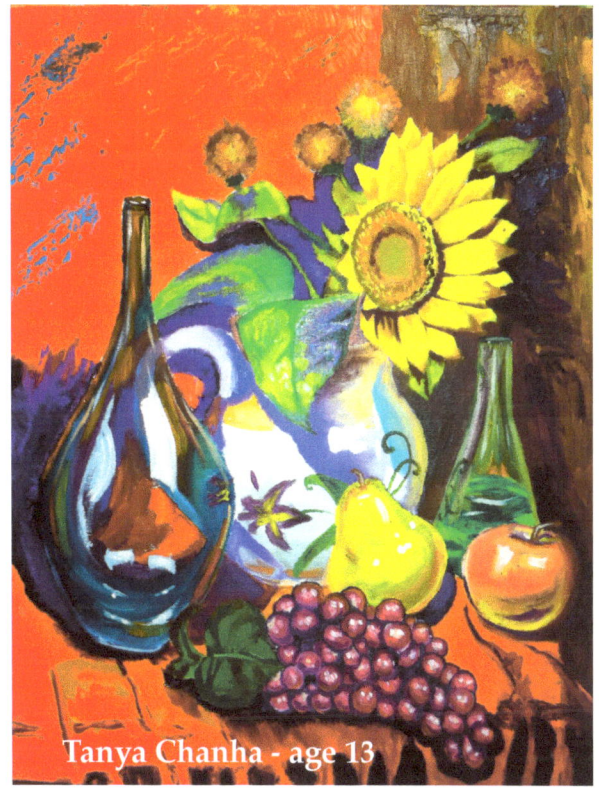

Tanya Chanha - age 13

Truck
Tree

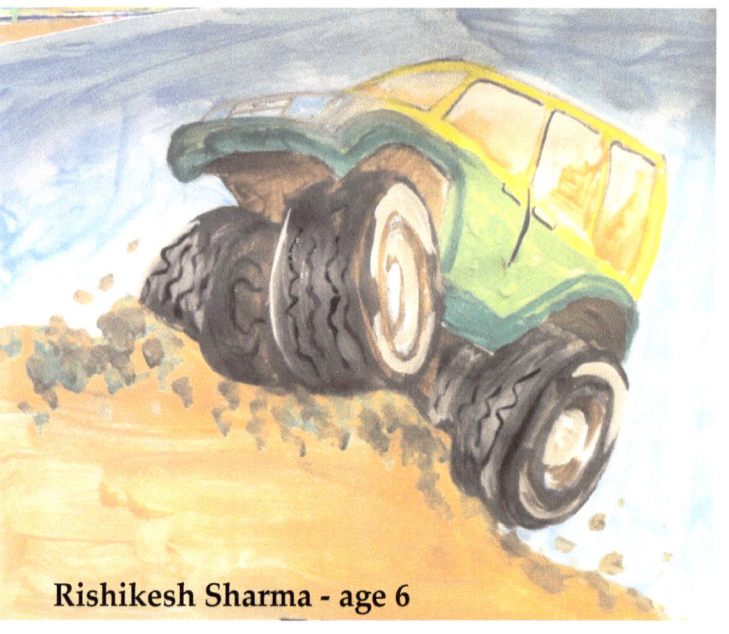

Rishikesh Sharma - age 6

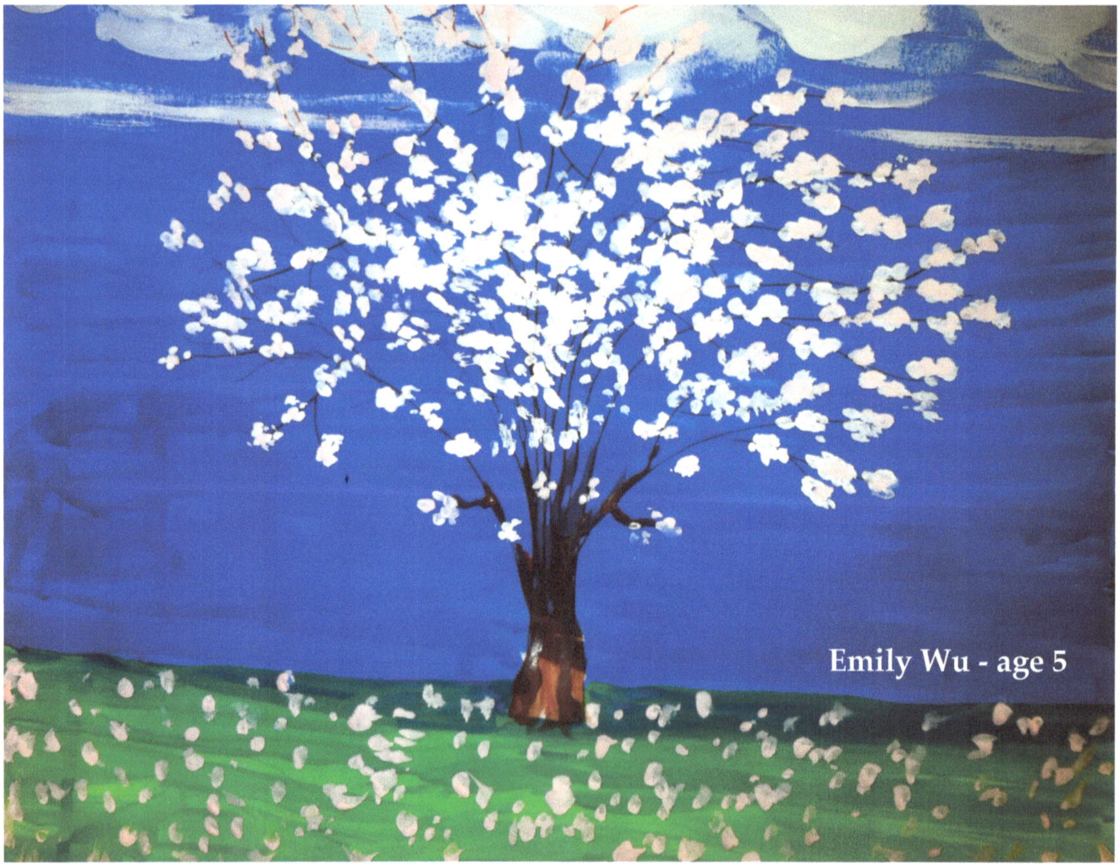

Emily Wu - age 5

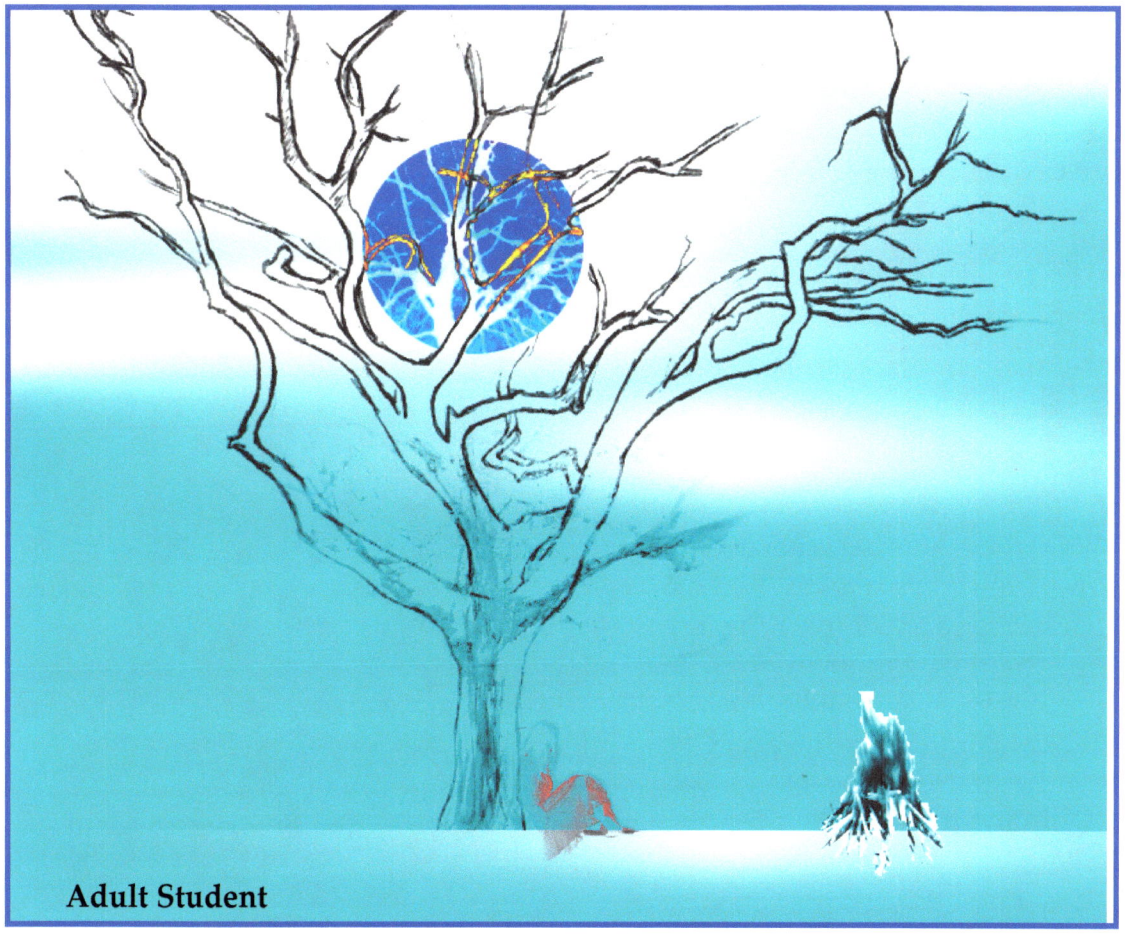

Adult Student

Watercolor painting of the truck and acrylic painting of the blossoming tree are triangle landscape compositions. Ask your child to find out triangles and ovals in these paintings.

When triangles in the painting with the truck are visible and may be found quickly, to find triangle in painting with the blossoming tree may be tricky. That is why, artist drew a trunk of the tree with branches without flowers on the right.

To paint this beautiful tree, your child should use acrylic paint: ultramarine blue color for the background and green color for the grass. After background will be completely dry, he or she needs to draw trunk with the crust of the tree with branches by dark brown sharpie similar to the drawing on the left. After that, he needs to paint this three by brown and orange acrylic paint and let it dry. The last step will include painting of white and pink flowers covering all branches similar to those as you can see on the blossoming tree painting.

Under-the-Sea Unicorn

Life Under-the-Sea is never ending children's creativity box. How many adventures waiting for them in unknown word of the ocean. Ask a child to make a story about Under-the-Sea. One of the first caracter can be this **Dolphin**, does not it?

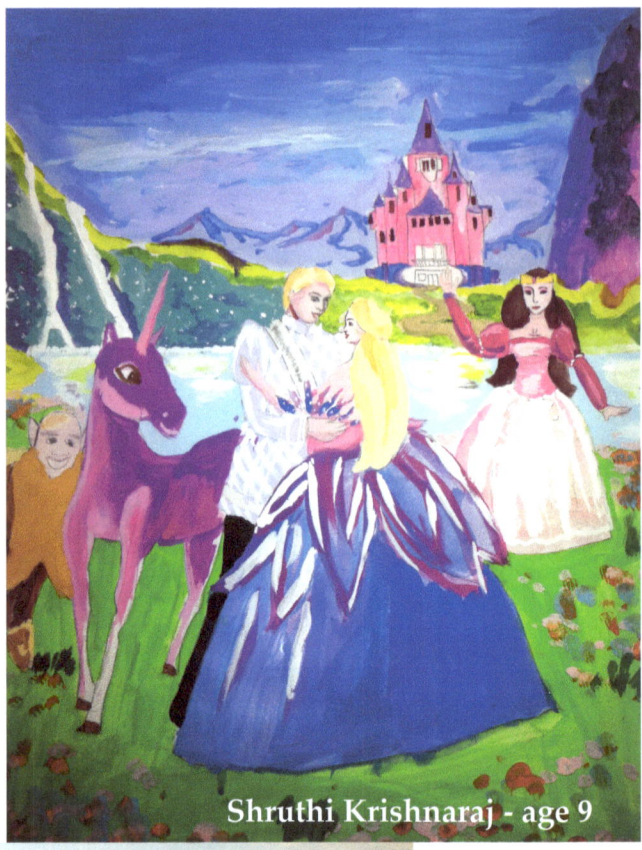

Shruthi Krishnaraj - age 9

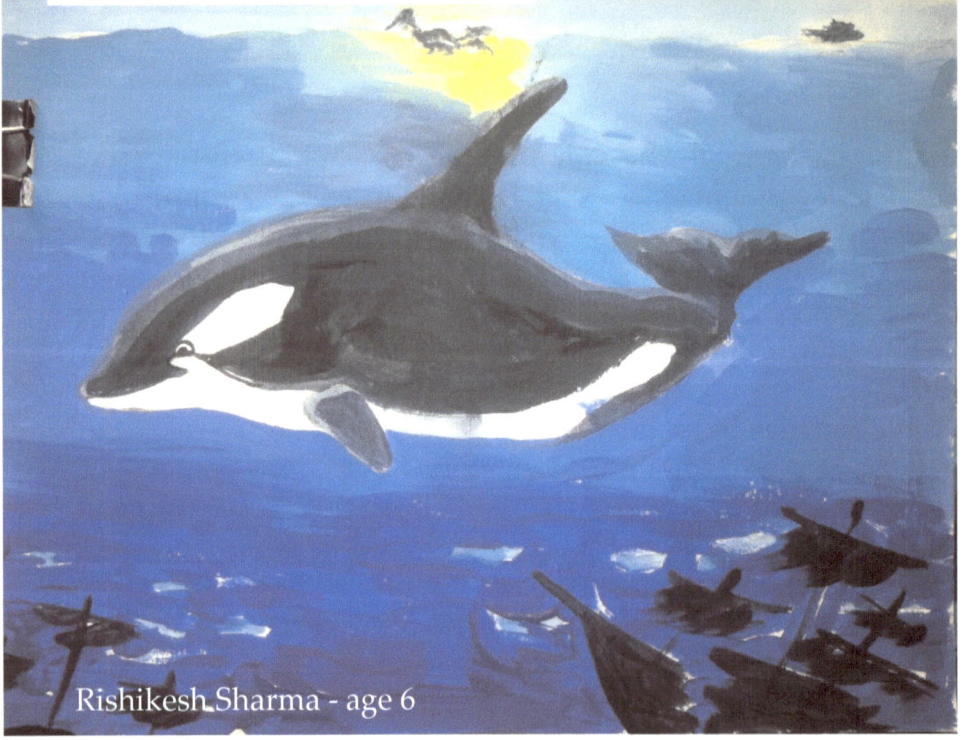

Rishikesh Sharma - age 6

Vegetables

Two pots surrounded by some vegetables may call young cooks for competition. Ask a child which ingredients he or she needs to add to the painting to prepare his or her favorite soup. We would like to know this recipe.

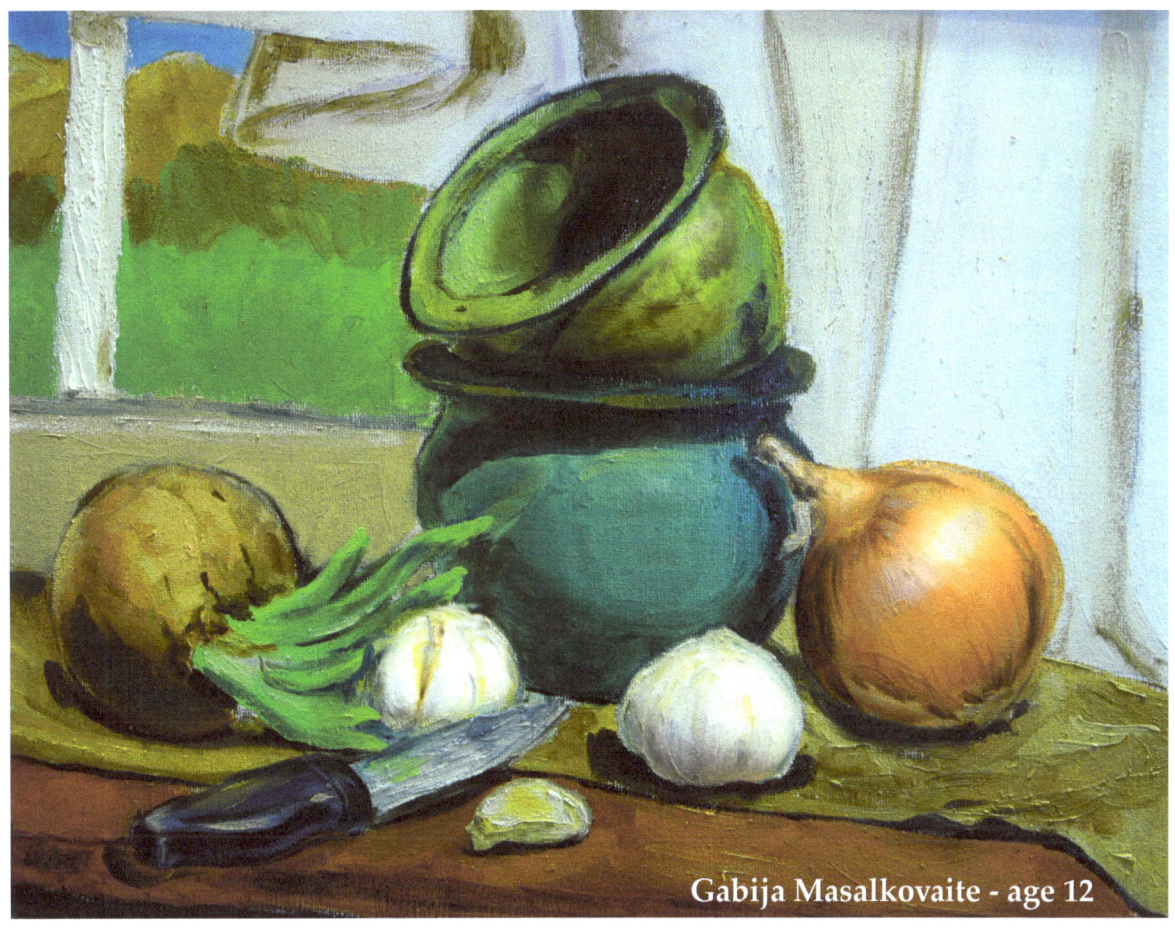

Gabija Masalkovaite - age 12

Wave
Watercolor

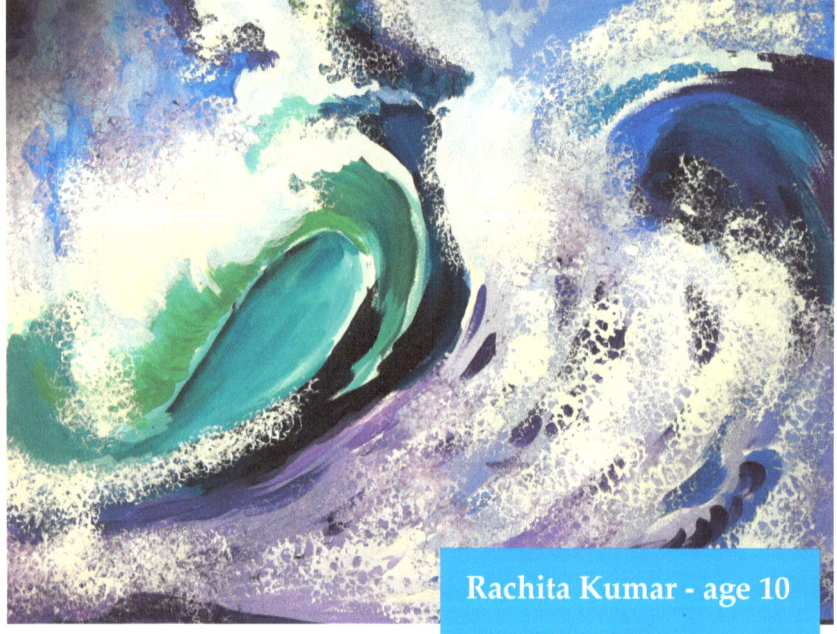

The painting(s) you see was created by watercolor technique. Using this media, your child will discover the excitement of color mixing and layering. Your child willingness to depict something may vary from any flower he or she likes to the seascape presented here and literally to any subject beyond this presentation. A variety of brushes may help create different strokes, which may be visible or not. Prior starting, he or she would need to paint entire drawing just by simple water. After that, a child would bring some water on a palette (plate) and add needed color(s). Then he would decide which color should be put on a paper. When one layer of background, for example, will be completely dry, a young artist may input another layer to indicate shadow. To learn more about this technique, it would be better to take a lesson in the art class.

Rachita Kumar - age 10

X-mas

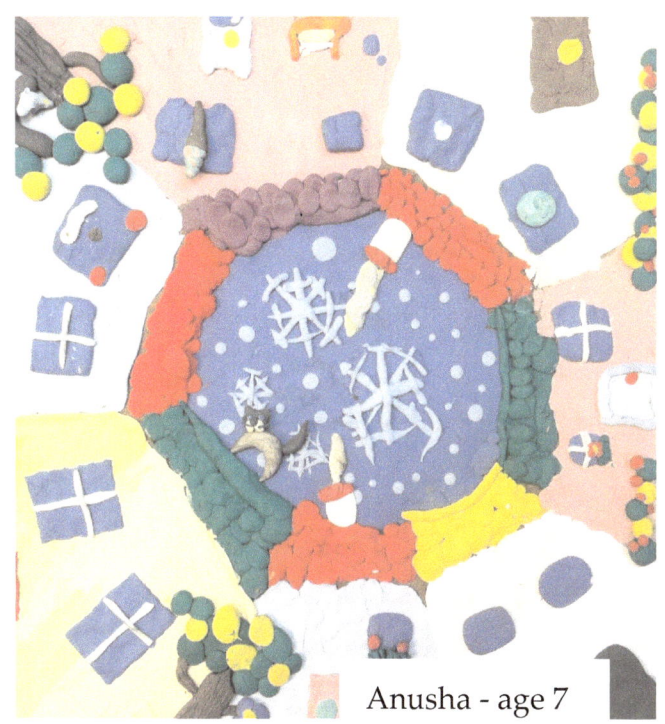

Anusha - age 7

On this page you will see the watercolor painting and clay composition. Both painting and clay compositions reflect winter. Ask a child to find X in both pictures. It is a believe that as more Xs he or she will find, then more presents a child will get on a Winter Holliday in this year in comparison with the previous one.

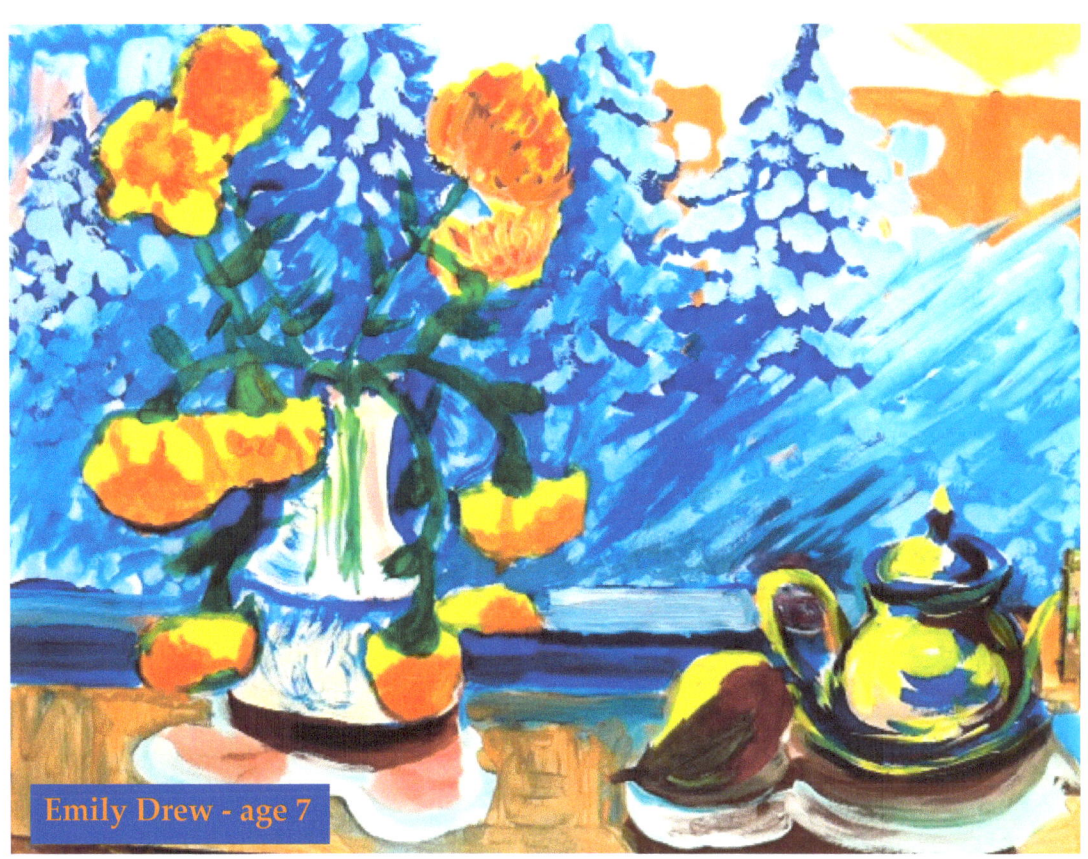

Emily Drew - age 7

Yellow

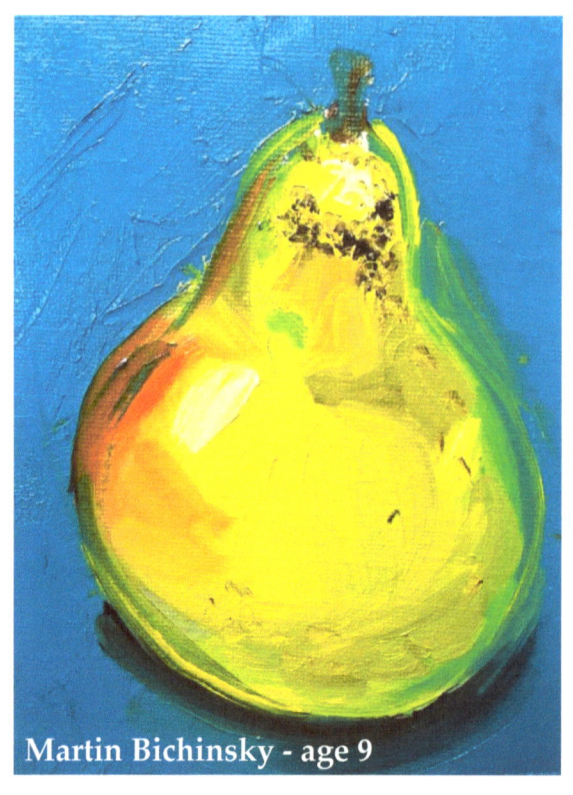

Martin Bichinsky - age 9

Oil painting of Yellow Pear represented on this page shows warm and juicy fruit. Ask your child about other fruits and vegetables which he or she may color by using yellow paint or by mixing this color with the another one (e.g., melon, lemon, orange, apple, corn, apricot). Let a child try to mix yellow acrylic paint with (1) orange; (2) red, (3) blue, and (4) green. So then he would have a chance to say which color would be best for coloring which fruit.

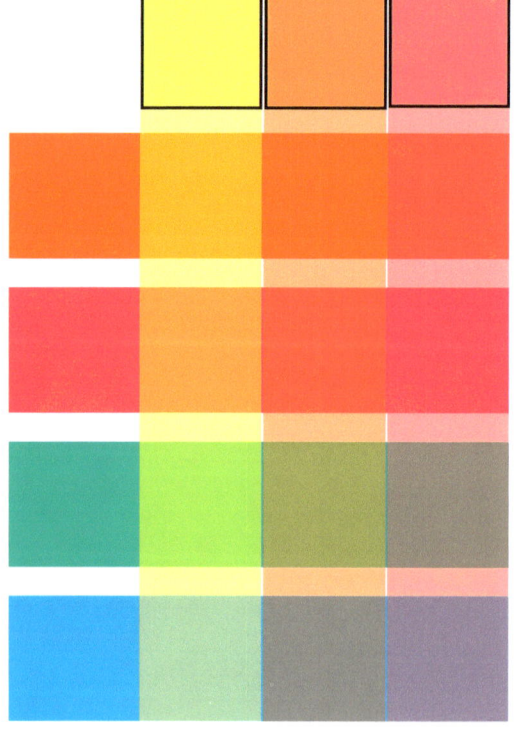

Zebra

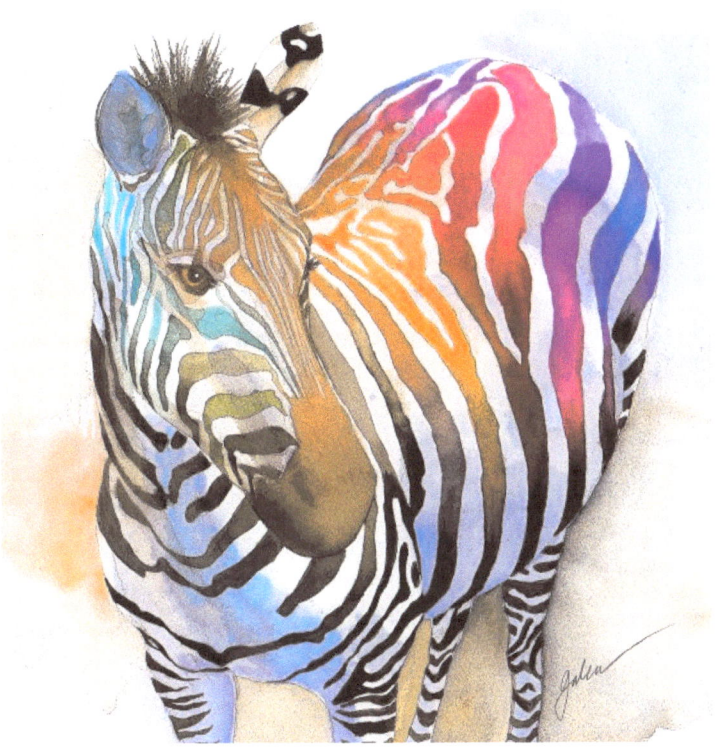

Adult Student

Z for Zebra. Young artist used watercolor technique to depict strips on the skin of a beautiful animal to underline its beauty. Ask a child to draw a rug with the similar strips and include multi colorful letters "Z" in between the strips. Child also may create design for dress or jacket presented on a page by using colorful strips and letter "Z" in different direction.

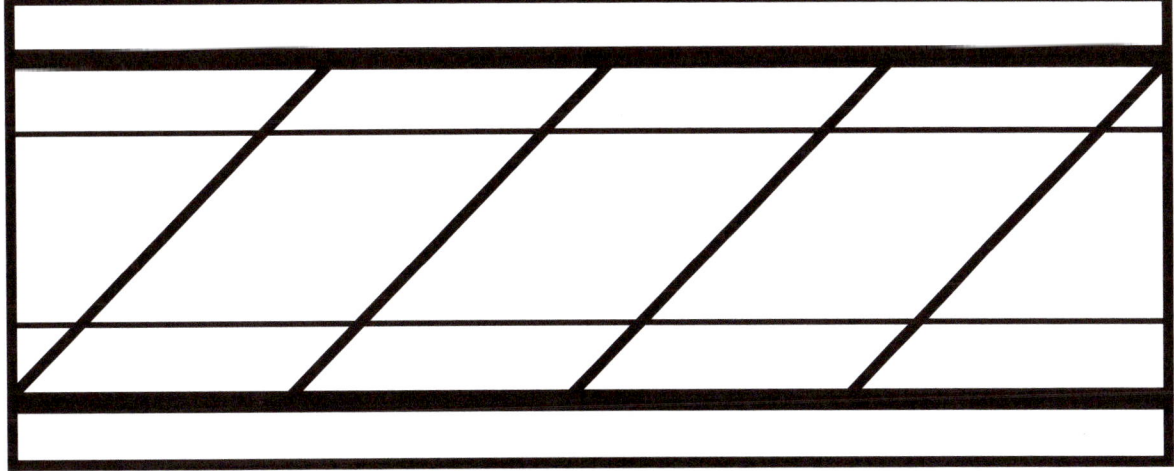

About Authors

Dr. Marina Bichinsky

I love art and can do everything possible and impossible by free-hands and digital art programs. I entered the pasture of visual arts 25 years ago and although my professional occupations and preferences have been changed, twisted, and extended during my life, they have been always associated with the fine art, graphic design, and illustration.

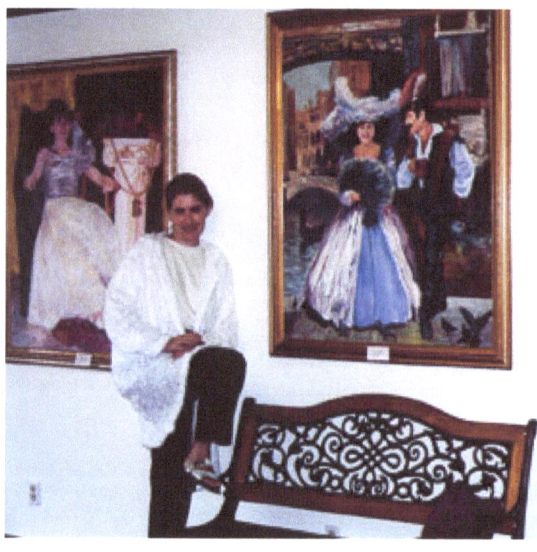

I was raised in an artistic family. My grandfather was a writer and journalists and my mother is an artist. As a child of five years old I was brought by my mom to Gulyaev's Art Studio and I am proud to say that this famous artist and master-teacher involved me in the marvelous world of fine art and led me through all steps of development knowledge and skills needed to be accomplishment artist.

Later in high-school, I was selected to participate in a federally-funded program for the Gifted and Talented in Visual and Performing Art School.

After graduating the high school, I won a huge competition and was admitted as a student of the Architectural department of the Kiev Architectural Civil University, where I spent another five years to study architectural concepts, forms, and structures while applying my art skills to exciting projects. Moving to the United States with my family, I took portfolio of my art and architec-

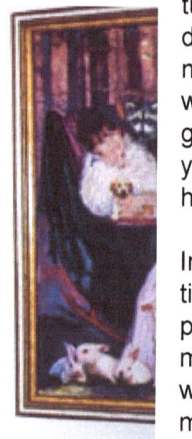

tural works, which opened doors for me and provided me with an opportunity to work as an architect and graphic artist since the first year of living in my new homeland (1993).

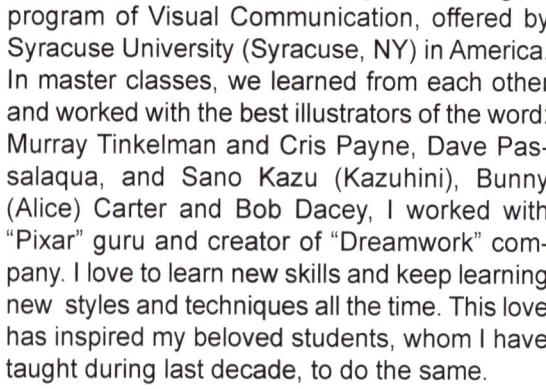

In 2001, I decided to continue my art education, and portfolio of works created in my native land provided me with an opportunity to be admitted and become one of most talented artists and illustrators, chosen by the director of the most extraordinary Master degree program of Visual Communication, offered by Syracuse University (Syracuse, NY) in America. In master classes, we learned from each other and worked with the best illustrators of the word: Murray Tinkelman and Cris Payne, Dave Passalaqua, and Sano Kazu (Kazuhini), Bunny (Alice) Carter and Bob Dacey, I worked with "Pixar" guru and creator of "Dreamwork" company. I love to learn new skills and keep learning new styles and techniques all the time. This love has inspired my beloved students, whom I have taught during last decade, to do the same.

There is no place for drilling, there is place for development own vision and creativity through excitement and fun.

I have traveled around the globe presenting my art in numerous exhibitions and have seen the most beautiful places of our planet. Reflections of my vision were presented on all five continents. I have completed illustrations to 7 books in the series of business word, which where written and published with my business partner Dr. Jane Goretskaya. I have also illustrated Dr. Goretskaya Anatomy of the World of Education textbook and some novels by other authors. Books in business series contain countless caricatures and cartoons on the most famous people of Silicon Valley, to reflect postmodern view of involving irony and parodies in daily life of organizations.

Graduating as a Doctor in Management in 2012, have applied what I has learned within the program to growth of my business in art school, where my colleagues and I are doing everything possible to teach students of different levels, age and experience to grow their talent and and make then succeed according to highest standards of academic curriculum within the studio program. Those students that want to continue their study in art colleges have an opportunity to create portfolio on the level required by the most prestige's American University.

Welcome to the Studio!

Dr. Marina Bichinsky

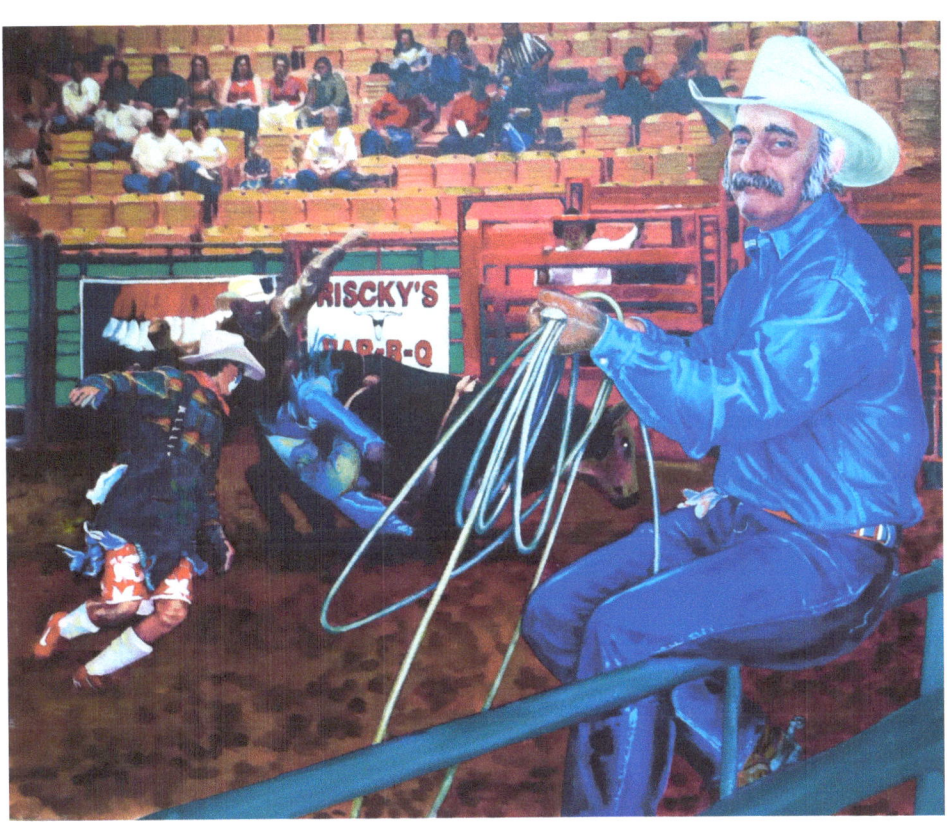

Marina Bichinsky, «Rodeo», 2008, oil on canvas

Dr. Jane Goretskaya

I entered the pasture of arts 30+ years ago and although my professional occupations and preferences have been changed, combined, replaced, and extended during my long life, they were always associated with arts.

I have studied fine art in Ukraine with the famous Ukrainian artist Matvey Gulyaev. My works brought from Europe have opened many doors for me. Just two months after arriving in Syracuse, NY, I was accepted everywhere I wanted to be, including Metropolitan School for the Arts, where I taught fine art courses and Museum of Science and Technology, where I created wall murals, slide-shows for planetarium, and books illustration. I was accepted with open arms by Murray Tinkelman, director of the most prestige's Master degree Visual Art program in Syracuse University, who selected only 20 artists-students each two years from around the world.

Within this program, I studied and worked with the most talented and famous American illustrators and after graduation as Master of Arts was immediately invited as a professor to teach Fashion Illustration in Cazenovia University,

Cazenovia, NY and later in other institutions to teach a variety of humanity courses, including World Culture and Arts, Cultural Diversity, Critical Thinking, Learning Skills and Technology, American Culture, and Social Media. With my partner Marina Bichinsky, we have opened art gallery in Carmel-by-the-Sea, where we created portraits and exposited our art works.

To teach at university level, I graduated as Doctor in Educational Leadership from University of Phoenix in 2007, where I am currently working as a professor in the College of Humanity. My Dissertation was about influence of Art Education and Distance Learning on students' academic achievements in elementary, middle, and high schools in California. The part of dissertation was about influence of Art Education and Distance Learning on development social and communication skills. In addition, I have wrote books and articles on educational, psychological, and organizational issues and have continued to be a partner with Marina Bichinsky in Living Art studio, when I perform as a Curriculum Developer of Fine Art program for teaching a variety of levels students and teaching them myself while dedicating my heard and skills to their success.

Welcome to the studio!

Dr. Jane Goretskaya

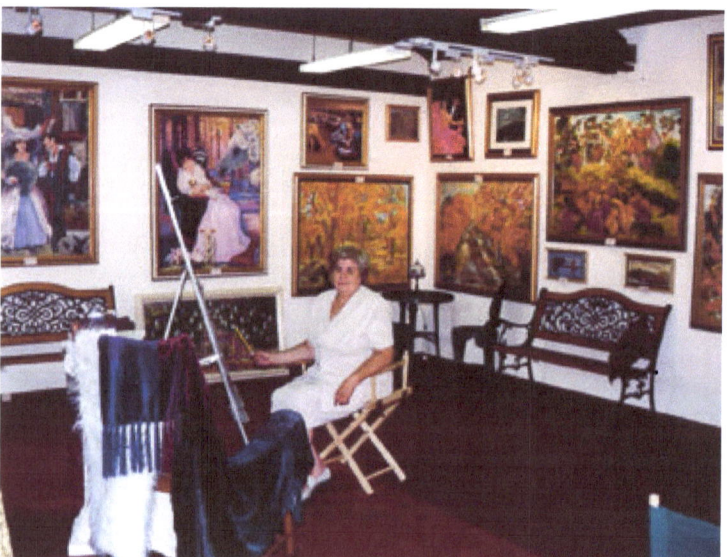

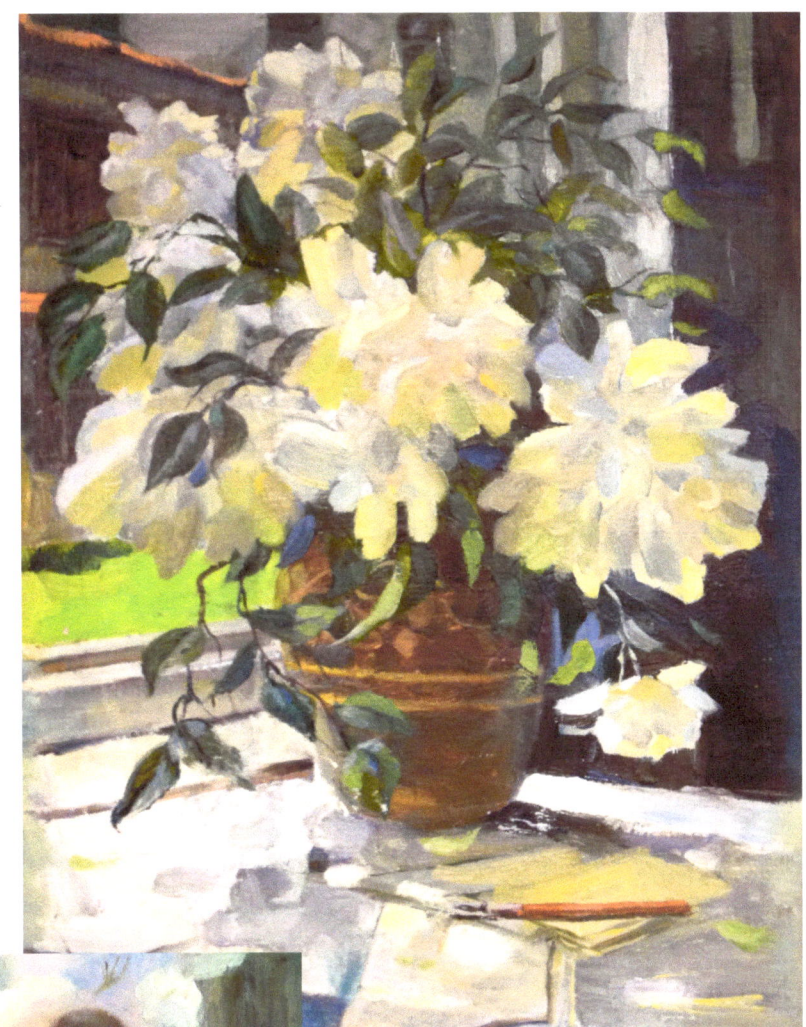

Jane Goretskaya, «White Flowers», 2008, oil on canvas

Jane Goretskaya, «Tea Party», 2010, oil on canvas

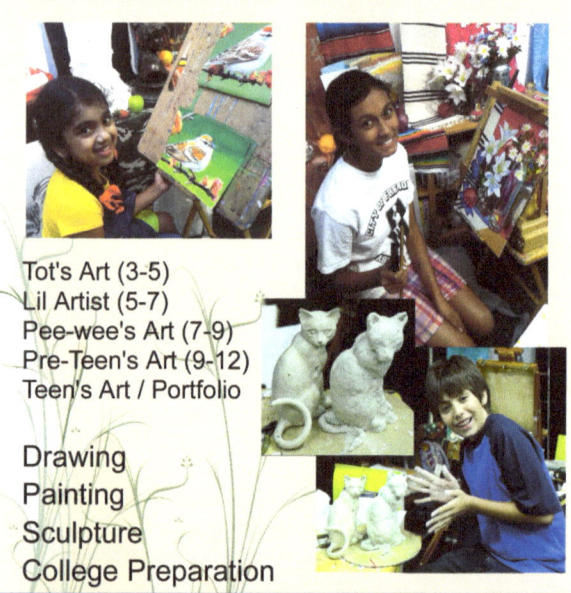
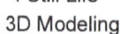
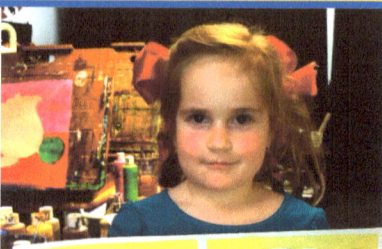
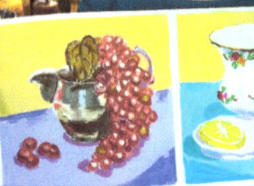
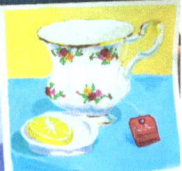
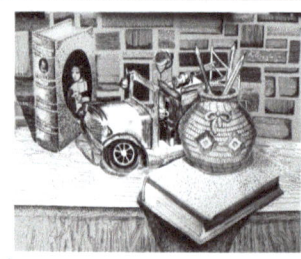
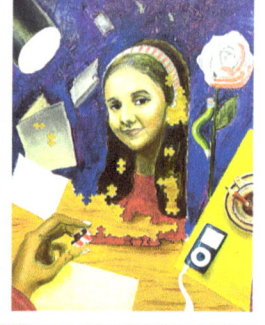
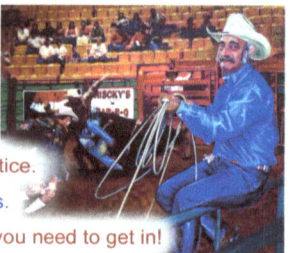